YOUR
ETERNAL
IDENTITY

Practicing the Principles of
A Spirit-Supplied Life

JULANNE DALKE

©2024 Julanne Dalke
Your Eternal Identity - Practicing the Principles of a Spirit-Supplied Life

eBook ISBN: 978-1-962570-92-3
Paperback ISBN: 978-1-962570-93-0
Hardcover ISBN: 978-1-962570-95-4
Ingram Spark ISBN: 978-1-962570-94-7
Library of Congress Control Number: 2024916449

Editor: N.J. Strickland
Cover Image: Adobe Stock
Cover Design: Angie Ayalya
Interior Design: Marigold2k

Publisher: Spotlight Publishing House™
https://SpotlightPublishingHouse.com

YOUR
ETERNAL
IDENTITY

Practicing the Principles of
A Spirit-Supplied Life

JULANNE DALKE

SPOTLIGHT
PUBLISHING HOUSE
Goodyear, Arizona

Testimonials

"Julanne's work is deep, profound and clear. She is a fun-loving and empowered woman who loves to support others in finding their way through life. Her work is truly liberating."
—Dawn Lianna, M.A. NLP
Owner of Intuitive Callings Publishing and Training Company

"Julanne Dalke's wisdom, wit and wealth of knowledge are matched only – perhaps – by her creativity, charisma and compassion. Julanne and her vast, creative, spiritual toolkit have been of enormous value to me every time we have interacted, often at critical junctures and transitions in my life. Be prepared. Working with Julanne will change your life…way, way, way for the better."
—Laura Jones, Author of *Six Degrees to Your Dreams*, Editor's Choice Award recipient, iUniverse

"Julanne has personally helped many reach an inner connection through soulful connection and inspired writings. My life has magnanimously improved by her guidance and wisdom!"
—Melanie Payton, business owner and satisfied meditation student

"This book is a call to action. If you are hungry for an opportunity to embrace change, take responsibility for your own life actions and be transformed, this book is for you. Simple, expert advice rests on every page. It reads like a meditation with real life stories proving that you get what you think about. The message is simple. The

examples sound. It helped me realize that I have the power over my own destiny as I apply the principles outlined in Your Eternal identity."
—Julie Jin, B.A, RMT, ACM, Minister Rays of Healing, Acasma & Johrei Practitioner, Angel Card Mastery & Guide, psychic/medium intuitive, internationally accredited with American Council of Holistic Healers and WMA.

"**Your Eternal Identity** is a profound guide for spiritual seekers, offering a pathway to a happy, healthy, high-performance and fulfilled life. The author gently leads readers to recognise their true spiritual essence—a constant state of love, clarity, wisdom and pure potential beneath the innocent yet limiting habits of the personal mind. She encourages us to pause and be still, reminding us, *"As you develop a stronger connection to Divine Wisdom, you will further strengthen your intuition and develop a higher purpose of spiritual clarity. Without resistance, in the lucidness of a sound mind, you will find yourself in the midst of your Eternal Identity"*.
Denise Holland—Transformative Coach, Speaker, PlayFreely®— Spiritual Awareness in Sports

Table of Contents

When You Wish Upon a Star

When you wish upon a star
Makes no difference who you are
Anything your heart desires
Will come to you

If your heart is in your dream
No request is too extreme
When you wish upon a star
As dreamers do

Like a bolt out of the blue
Fate steps in and sees you through
When you wish upon a star
Your dreams come true

Music by Leigh Harline
Lyrics by Ned Washington
Performed by Cliff Edwards as Jiminy Cricket
(with chorus and orchestra)
Written for the 1940 Disney movie, "Pinocchio"
Recorded in 1939
Released on February 9, 1940
Winner of the Academy Award for Best Music
(Original Song)

Foreword

I am an entrepreneur, speaker, author, and connector with over 23 years of experience in the internet and event industry. I am the owner and founder of the iNETreprenuer Network and advocate for the Art of Connection Movement. iNETreprenuer Network is the parent company of iNETrepreneur Radio, iNETrepreneur Referrals, Network Together, and iNETrepreneur Publishing. My mission is to celebrate and connect entrepreneurs, influencers, experts, authors, and speakers through various platforms and outlets that provide visibility, exposure, and income opportunities.

I am also a proud Marine, a TEDx panelist, and a 7x #1 international bestselling author. I have published works at the Library of Congress, and I host the iNETrepreneur Radio Show, where I interview inspiring and successful entrepreneurs from different fields and backgrounds. I publish the iNETrepreneur Magazine, a quarterly publication that features stories, tips, and insights from our community of entrepreneurs. I also organize and host in-person and virtual events, such as the iNetwork Expo, that bring together hundreds of business owners and professionals for networking, learning, and collaboration. I am passionate about coaching, mentoring, and empowering others to achieve their goals and make a difference.

I met Julanne as a contributing author in the international best seller, *The Art of Connection, 365 Days of Gratitude Quotes by Entrepreneurs, Business Owners and Influencers*. Her philosophy mirrors my own, as she feels it is important to be inspired by the light and love in service to others. Writing is a profound expression that reverberates with the social bonds that create a significant impact on the lives of others.

Julanne is a visionary of bliss and creativity born out of a need to survive her beloved husband's experiences with heart disease, cancer, and loss of eyesight. She spends very little time writing about tragedy, and a lot of time solving problems that bring benefits to the reader as a result. Her goal is to demonstrate how to emerge as a person with confidence, passion, and divine purpose. I appreciate it that her values are sound. She is a storyteller of true life and allows her vulnerability to show up on every page.

> *"I was a hider for years,"* she told me. *"From childhood I lived under conditional love, a people pleaser to the core. I held tight to unnecessary fears that held me back. I was actually hospitalized as a result of anxiety. But as an adult I gave myself permission to dream a new dream, and create the future I wanted for myself. I soon became limitless. Every time I questioned myself, every time I was afraid to fall, I tapped into my inner Voice that told me the truth. I am worthy to receive anything I ask for. The thoughts you bring to mind are the first step towards liberation."*

Throughout the chapters of *Your Eternal Identity*, she is meticulous and intentional in her quest to help people open up their true potential by aligning with the Divinity within. Every chapter offers an inspirational quote along with an affirmation supporting four principles: change, adaptation, transformation and self-realization.

To quote her,

> *"What I am going through now is part of my soul's process. I am on a golden path. The choices I make now are important. I know the sun is shining on my intentions now for personal growth and life lessons."*

This book will open your eyes to what it takes to change channels in your life for the better, by focusing on what is going right, not wrong. Julanne provides practical exercises rooted in personal stories of success by applying appreciation and gratitude in the face of adversity. As you begin to implement her processes and teachings into your life, you will find freedom from lack, fear, anxiety and dis-ease.

> *"As you learn to live with your eternal identity, you begin to identify and become friends with your spiritual nature and apply this power to your everyday life. I found my energy levels improved. I felt lighter, and happier, more and more in love with life."*

As I read through this book I was reminded of the trials and tribulations I have faced in my own life. No one is exempt. So often I felt trapped in my own circumstances. There were moments when I questioned my own sanity, asking myself why I would undertake such ambitious tasks. In reading this book I was inspired to create my own confidence… a fearless effort that allows me to pursue my passions and dreams without holding back.

> *"You might wish that you could snap your fingers, and all your problems will disappear. On the contrary, as you get honest with yourself, you will gain clarity on how and why you might want to embrace change. The journey may or may not be easy. It depends on your willingness to implement new perspectives."*

Julanne gives you the tools to be emotionally invested and asks you to live on purpose, with purpose, and not by default.

This book has brought value to my life and will bring value to the world and to the clients the reader serves. Most people want to attract a soulmate, friends, a dream college, a more appealing physical appearance, financial stability and peace of mind. That is why I am thrilled to have the opportunity to write the foreword for *Your Eternal Identity,* to be in light and love in service to others. Together we can create a ripple of positive thinking that will expand into the whole world by applying affirmative thoughts. I am delighted you are about to learn from someone I would call a master at their craft... living a life in alignment with the Victor within!

Robert W. Jones
Sincerely,
Robert W. Jones

Founder & Chairperson, Art of Connection, iNETrepreneur Network, Network Together, LLC.
Email: robert@networktogether.net
Join us at an
Event: https://business.inetrepreneurnetwork.com/events/calendar/
iNETrepreneur Magazine: http://inetrepreneurmagazine.com/
iNETrepreneur Radio: http://inetrepreneurradio.com/

Overview

An important new beginning is at hand. I know that you want to bring clarity and wisdom to the world. Find your voice and let your wisdom shine! You can move toward the completion of your desires and dreams as you open up to the complete truth of your eternal wisdom, talents and abilities. Take the risk of believing in yourself. You have all the resources you need and the unlimited source of divine Supply at your disposal. As you learn to love and value yourself without limitation, tender, loving treatment toward yourself and others will come to you in wonderful and unexpected ways. Let your light shine!

Nearly every revolutionary change in the history of human progress came about because someone questioned a time-honored belief or tradition. The question reveals a new truth, a new way of doing things, and a new standard of ethical and moral behavior. Please keep an open mind.

In the course of your life, you will come across individuals who presume to know what is best for you. It usually starts with your parents! No surprise there, right?

The problem is, your Eternal Identity is an elusive concept. Many inherently feel they must define themselves by what they do and what others perceive is best. From an early age, children are under the influence of a relatively small selection of roles and consistent character traits modeled by others. Those traits seldom accurately represent your own intrinsic sense of self.

The confusion surrounding your true nature is further compounded by society, who consistently asks you to suppress your emotions, intellect and spiritual vibrancy. Society is in favor of trying to glean from you whatever they are reaching for outside of themselves. People often expect *you* to change so *they* can feel better. There's a lot of shame and blame that goes with this concept and it never feels good for either party involved. Think of yourself looking into a mirror. Would you speak to yourself like you sometimes speak to others?

Do you want to know a secret? Your Eternal Identity lies in imagining yourself to be in alignment with your spiritual twin. As you do, you will lose the blame, shame, insincerity and grief.

The awareness that society has concluded about you cannot compare with the powers of understanding and intuition that already exist within you. From birth, you are blessed with a yearning to follow your path of personal alignment. You were born with a Wisdom that cannot be unlearned. It exists and can be rekindled along your growing path because it is a gift given to you by a loving Presence that accompanied you on your journey to this earthly plane.

You are, in truth, a being of light, pure positive energy inhabiting a physical body. Yet for all its permanence, people sometimes ignore this incredible element of Eternal Identity. It is when you do not use your inborn Wisdom that you begin to doubt your personal truths. What you instinctively know is true in your heart is invariably guaranteed. You can discover how attractive and useful self-trust can be when you grow into the power of your internal understanding.

If you imagine your intuition has a voice, you might ask that voice what it's trying to tell you. Following the advice you find through the power of your own speech could lead to making decisions based on what the inner reaches of your soul desires, rather than on external factors that tend to influence you.

When we acknowledge and then practice the power of the voice within, our innate luminosity and Divinity, we cannot help but live an authentic and masterful life.

The voice within is not subject to the influences of the outside world, which means that it will never demand that you surrender your free will. Your Eternal Identity will not counsel you to act in opposition to your values. You benefit from inspiration when you open yourself to it. Wisdom acts as a companion to discernment and offers you the ability to identify blessings in disguise.

When you are unsure of who to trust, how to answer your own questions, or come to terms with what it is you really want, ask for answers that lie dormant in your inner self. Your *Spiritual* Companion knows where you are going and understands where you are coming from. Divine Wisdom is activated by faith and is yours simply by being born. It is your Divine birthright.

In the whole of your existence, no outside force you will ever encounter will contribute as much to your ability to do what you need to do and be who you want to be as that of your guiding, inner light. It is fired by the Divine Mind. By inviting it, you surrender your growing consciousness to the greater Source and discover the true extent of your strength and power. As you heed this Wisdom with conviction and confidence, the mosaic of your life will unfold with ease and grace. The fears that hold you back will be dissolved.

This will pave the way for you to fulfill your truest potential. Align yourself with true authority, your Eternal Identity.

Realize your true purpose by mastering your own mind. Be true to yourself and let your light shine forth. As you hold this book in your hands, tap into the experience. Personal, valuable information specific to *your* needs will be revealed. I will show you how you can uncover your true Higher Self, your wise Inner Companion, your Eternal Identity.

It doesn't take years of practice to become free from limiting behaviors. Recognize that it has been fear holding you back from living a stress-free life. Most of us live with unfounded anxiety as a result of looking for approval outside ourselves. (Can you place a name on who that might be?) The fact is, nobody cares as much about you and the way you live your life as you might think.

I was a hider for years. I didn't want to let on that I was a victim of abuse. I blamed myself. I berated myself. I lived with the shame that held me hostage. Whatever it is you are hiding from, it's never too late to forgive yourself for being human. Dust off your shoes and move on to a more joyous life experience. You can't go back and redo the past, but you can begin to live a happy and carefree life.

Your history doesn't have to define your destiny. By being alert and consciously applying positive attributes to every moment in appreciation, you will begin to let go of everything that has been holding you back.

"In the moment" is the best time to make that simple and powerful decision. I often ask myself how it took me so long to realize that I could use my imagination to change my behavior. What I found is that I was blocked in fear instead of love. Take courage, and ask yourself these questions:

Are you at war with how you truly feel?

Are you being influenced by your most intimate circles?

Are you living your life to be accepted by your parents, peers, wife, husband, children, co-workers, or society in general?

Do you feel stifled? Stuck?

Are you willing to make up your mind to feel safe rather than attacked?

Are you ready to allow yourself to feel secure rather than judged?

Are you of a mind to allow yourself to feel calm instead of harassed?

Understand your spiritual nature and learn how to apply this power to your everyday life. By mastering thought and aligning with the Divine Source within you, you can free yourself from pain and release it. As you do, your energy levels will improve. Your stamina and courage will return. You will find yourself more and more in the flow of well-being.

I have learned that nothing outside of me can touch me. In some ways, I must have invited my fear or encouraged it in some sort of self-sabotage. Your natural state of being is Love. Trust yourself. You are the best friend you will ever have! Accept this as though it is your current reality. Believe it, affirm it, practice it and you will see it gain momentum in your quest to master life, your *own* life!

What does it mean to live with your Eternal Identity? What exactly IS your Eternal Identity?

Eternal Identity is the part of the human heart that carries a frequency of intuition and emotion. Granted, you cannot *see* Consciousness, but in its purity it is capable of transcending fear-based thoughts. It is faith that points to the Presence of an absolute Other. Some might call it your conscience, Spirit, or your mind's eye. It is an inner feeling or voice viewed as a guide to the rightness or wrongness of one's behavior. It's a nudge. It's the promptings of guardian angels. It's a red alert. It's fight or flight. An inner guide. An awareness of and response to our surroundings while we are awake. It's the distinction between the natural you and the non-material side of you. It is a transpersonal state of consciousness *beyond* the limits of physical identity. It is your Eternal Identity.

The power of discernment exists within each and every one of us. You are an extension of the same benevolent well-being who speaks to you as Higher Consciousness throughout the pages of this book. You can and will learn to honor this incredible element of Self. When you use your inborn Wisdom, you cannot doubt your personal truths. Would you agree that we often doubt ourselves?

The Inner Voice is not subject to the influences of the outside world. The Wisdom inside you is available to you as a Stream of Consciousness. It is revealed to you as you listen, through language and symbols that you can understand and employ. Spirit uses all kinds of ways to alert you to messages: music, nature, feelings of warmth, joy, satisfaction, friendships, business relationships, family and children, to name a few. It can also alert you to various dangers such as abuse, terror, sabotage, unrest, accidents and injury.

Your Eternal Identity knows where you are going and understands where you are coming from. It is your personal connection to the Universal Mastermind. While reading and applying the promptings outlined in this book, you access the ability to tap into the true extent of your inner power. In the beginning, I had a vision…you can, too. Be open. Wake up as you begin to align with the Divine.

There is no gap between you and your Eternal Identity.

It is who you truly are.

Glossary

This book will activate your faith in the principles aimed toward spiritual pursuits. While I have always respected traditional religions, it is my intention to keep this book non-denominational. I would like to offer my definitions of common words used throughout the text.

Eternal Identity, Spiritual Companion, Guide, Presence, Divine Mind, Grace, Supply, Hero, Divine Inspiration, God, Inner Being, Omnipresence, Avatar, Wisdom, Inspiration	The word *Love* is used by different names. These words are used interchangeably to define what I consider to be Holy names for *Love*.
Affirmation	Emotional support and encouragement.
Faith	Complete trust or confidence based on spiritual understanding, rather than physical proof.
Imagination	Forming new ideas and concepts not present to the senses.
Meditation	An act of quieting the mind.
Prayer	A solemn request for help from a supernatural source.
Synchronicity	A simultaneous occurrence of events which appear significantly related, but have no discernable casual connection.

Introduction

(or view my message on YouTube)
https://www.youtube.com/watch?v=wOKyv8NrZC8&t=2s

Dear Reader,

The purpose of *Your Eternal Identity* is to help you get solid on four Principles: *Transformation, Change, Adaptation* and *Self-Realization*.

Throughout the text, I will provide tutorials to gain access to insights proven to be effective in these areas. Each chapter can be read alone or in sequence, according to your needs.

Your Eternal Identity demonstrates in what ways my personal experience has taught me how easy it is to align with a divine energy. You will learn to believe that you can do what I have done as you embrace and apply the messages throughout these chapters. The *Change* I often refer to has its source in mental and emotional security, together with understanding the deeper meanings of life.

The word *Love* is used by different names: Eternal Identity, Spiritual Companion, Guide, Presence, Divine Mind, Grace, Supply, Hero, Divine, Inspiration, Inner Being, Omnipresence, Avatar, Wisdom and Inspiration. These words are used interchangeably to define what I consider to be Holy names for Love.

You might wish that you can snap your fingers and all your problems will disappear. On the contrary. Working toward the four Principles outlined in the first paragraph is going to take effort. As you get honest with yourself, you will gain clarity on how and why you might want to embrace *Change*. The journey may or may not be easy. It will depend on your readiness and willingness to implement new perspectives. We will focus on a positive outcome in all chapters. As you become emotionally invested, expect life-changing results. Doing this work is *your* choice.

This expedition called life will never provide you with a destination. With each day that unfolds, you have another opportunity to affirm an ongoing *lifestyle*.

You will find freedom in the principles outlined in the following chapters. Never give in, never give up as you become an active participant in your own life!

Practicing the Principles of a Spirit-Driven Life

Principle 1: Transformation

Transformation begins as a metamorphosis. As we grow into our bodies from infants to old age, a change of form inevitably takes place. By nature, we become the person we intend either by default or on purpose, but we constantly change into a completely different person by natural and supernatural laws. This transformation occurs internally and externally.

At times, transformation can be sudden, as in the loss of someone or something special to us. There are a myriad of emotions that result. Even though we need to be acutely aware of things we have no control over, we still have to take responsibility for our own actions. We can change our thoughts, and thus our actions, by conscious choice. We can lean on benevolent Wisdom to answer the most important questions we dare to ask. With the help of the Source within, you will learn how to create your own transformation.

Principle 2: Change

The purpose of *change* is to help you identify patterns moving in or out of your experience that may not be working. Letting go of those that don't work can help you become your best self.

At the beginning of every chapter, you are asked to *imagine yourself* speaking *to* yourself to truly hear your own thoughts. Once you understand what you're *really* saying to yourself, you can choose a different mindset through the use of affirmations.

Affirmations are a powerful tool in creating the kind of life you wish to experience. It is well known from scientific resources that it takes 21 days or 3 weeks to create a new habit. Affirmations are always created in the present tense by using first person "I" statements.

Thoughts are things and creating them more consciously allows you to create new and better habits or patterns in your life. In this way, you become the captain of your own ship, as it were, sailing through life at the helm. Wouldn't you rather be at the helm instead of at the mercy of life's storms? You may not be able to control the storm, but you CAN control how you think about the storm.

Perhaps you've heard of the yin and yang symbol. If not, it originated in ancient Chinese philosophy and shows a balance between two opposite elements. The original image shows dark and light portions of half a circle, but slightly overlapping into the other half. Each half describes opposite but interconnected forces and phenomena of life. Examples are typically in pairs, such as day and night, light and dark, hot and cold, good and bad, full moon and new moon, positive and negative, and so on. One cannot exist without the other. These elements coexist in all of nature and create the duality of our life on earth.

The symbol is meant to represent the need for the balance of opposite forces and change. Yin is black and associated with the moon, the feminine or shadow side of life, such as the mysterious. Yang is white and associated with the sun, the masculine side of life where things are more out in the open. Neither is more important or more powerful than the other. Both are needed in equal parts for harmony to exist.

In the yin cycle, most of the action happens under the radar. This is a great time to adopt a mindset of reflection, intuition and incubation. This allows you to chill out, breathe into your inner energy and listen to the still small voice within. Yin cycles often call you to be passive. I encourage you to be aware of the difference between yin and yang and be willing to be transformed by a readiness to embrace and invite change.

Principle 3: Adaptation

As you adjust to new conditions, you are able to make minor changes and attract unique and new situations.

A yang cycle calls for a more active approach with adaptation toward purposeful maneuvers. You can *imagine yourself* improving your thoughts with the use of the guided affirmation noted at the beginning of each chapter. By using your own credibility, you can create a new beginning, one that more closely reflects significant inner and outer change. All you need is already part of you. As you start paying more attention to your life, you will know which cycle you are in and can release any resistance to moving through it.

Principle 4: Self-Realization

After a few stories and examples in each chapter, I am going to ask you to illuminate your imagination. We will repeat positive affirmations as a mantra you can employ repeatedly. This will help you create new ideas and concepts to apply to your quest for *Self-Realization*.

Our minds have the ability to be creative and resourceful. The part of the mind that imagines things opens up alternatives and possibilities and guides your decision-making by creating a more favorable scenario. Many of the feelings I have had about the lack of success were, in fact, my failure to imagine myself as being capable of changing my mind to reflect inner and outer change.

To tap into the imagination activates our Divine power at its Source. Many times I apply a fictional affirmation to form a more favorable outcome. This aim toward my goals has served me well. Some have called this "acting as if" something were true until it actually does become true in your life.

You can, indeed, create a bridge between fact and reality. The imagination has the capacity to restore hope where there once was no escape or reprieve. It opens up alternatives and possibilities and guides your decision-making by playing those decisions out in your mind. I will show you how to apply alternative forms of awareness by activating emotion and *imagination*. This will support, supplement, and return you to the four Principles to life: *Transformation, Change, Adaptation* and *Self-Realization.*

You can expect the voice of your Eternal Identity to reveal itself as you listen to and apply the principles outlined in this book. Source will never ask you to surrender your free will or counsel you to act in opposition to your values. Be assured that you are never asked to give up your religious preferences. The Wisdom inside you will speak to you as a Stream of Consciousness. It is revealed through the language and symbols that you understand and employ, sometimes without even knowing how or why.

Your Eternal Identity is inspired by the Higher Consciousness that belongs to all of us. You will find yourself letting go of the notion that you are less qualified than those who raised you. The teachers who had an influence on you. The business associates who steered you in the direction of *their* dreams. You have the Wisdom inside of you that is the Source of YOUR discernment. There is an inner and outer relationship outlined in every circumstance in life. We are relational beings. As you master thought, you master life within those relationships.

I have discovered how to be my own best friend and advocate and look at most circumstances with honesty and integrity. As a result of some pretty tragic episodes, I made a *conscious decision* to create my own destiny on purpose and not by default. As you apply the principles laid out in this book, you can expect to experience similar success. As with any new idea, or one you are already familiar with and want to implement toward your own well-being, you will find that it takes practice. Nobody gets it right the first time.

I am entering the golden years now. Am I remiss? No! I appreciate every experience I have learned from and leave little to regret. Have

I made mistakes? Yes! This is why I recently opted for a life review. I learned a lot about myself as a result of writing this book. I *finally* left the shame, doubt, criticism, remorse and guilt behind. I have learned how to forgive myself and others. I will show you how you can, too.

I offer you my own life experiences. Some of this material will resonate with you and prompt you to take a closer look at how you want to live *your* life. Wait no longer to step into your power. Find the courage to think and act on your own behalf. I give you my unwavering support by providing the tools you will need to find the courage to act.

When my mother-in-law died, I asked the universe: "Who will pray for me now?"

I will. I will also pray for *you*. Have faith! I know you can do it!

Love and blessings,
Julanne Dalke
Your Eternal Identity

Imagine

Having the power within that is greater
than that which comes from the world.

Affirmation

I have all the power I need to create the destiny I desire.
Magic happens when I live in consciousness
and my eternal truth.

Chapter 1

Under the Influence of Love

(or view my message on YouTube)
https://www.youtube.com/watch?v=emJ3Gu7SPA0

L ove in action has many names.

Never before have there been so many deliberate creators who are embracing the concept that they have control over their own future by practicing personal alignment with their Eternal Identity. At no time before has the power of being under the influence of the Inner Hero been exposed to bear the truth that it is. Not ever have you acknowledged the content of your emotional guidance system to the degree you do now. Do you think the discovery of this realization is paramount? I sure do, and it starts with Love.

Love has many names and comes in many forms. Love is an intense feeling of deep affection.

Think of the way you felt when your children or grandchildren were born—a miracle of life and you were witness to it! In an instant, you became deeply committed and connected to this newborn baby. In the first moment you held her in your arms, an unbreakable bond was formed between the two of you. If you feel like I did, you felt a profoundly tender and passionate connection. I immediately formed a warm, personal attachment and deep affection for a blessed and miraculous life. This experience is just one form of Love.

Love encompasses a range of strong and positive emotional and mental states, of course, and goes beyond the sphere of elation. It includes responsibility, trust, empathy, sympathy, sublime virtue and established habits formed in the deepest interpersonal affection. It means respect, value, self-love and enacted emotions. You know in your bones that Love is not a feeling alone, but a tactile sense that propels you into the world of action.

Feel excitement about the adventure you have been exposed to on life's journey. Embrace it!

The Love that is transferred to you through your Eternal Identity is undeniable. There is a love that you were born with. It is not contingent upon the family you were born into. It does not depend upon the life experiences you have had to negotiate. It is not based upon the contrast you have been exposed to. This Love is yours and yours alone. It can never be taken away from you. Its value is so important that it will carry you through life's most severe and dire straits. The value of your Eternal Identity is unfathomable.

It is available to you whether you invite it or not. This Love will point you in the direction of your personal alignment and all that you want to experience in this lifetime. When you invite Love in its many forms and allow it, you receive guidance and direction. Freedom gives you reign to be all you can imagine life has to offer. As you listen to the promptings of your heart, different scenarios will appear. Choose without offering any resistance. Cease striving. Let go, be still, relax, set down your cares and seek the presence of Grace. Open your eyes and behold the wondrous things your Eternal Identity has in store for you!

Revel in your knowledge of what the non-physical is about. Express the understanding that you are an eternal being. Feel excitement about the adventures you have been exposed to on this life journey, and bask in the right set of circumstances. Love will show itself to you as you practice personal alignment with who you are. Begin to live from the inside out.

Be under your own influence. You don't need anybody to validate you or give you permission. You are capable of hearing the messages yourself. Imagine yourself practicing thoughts of worthiness, well-being, thoughts that just feel good. As you find balance, you will increase momentum and point yourself in the direction of whatever it is that you want. You have control over your own future when you practice personal alignment with Love. Embrace it, invite it, experience it, trust it.

Read the affirmations peppered throughout each chapter. They will give you a cheerful start. But just like when you are moving your furniture and belongings from a preexisting house to your new home, there will be chaos as you shake things up. You have to make a mess before you can get organized in the new location. So it is with the changes you make in your mind. The use of affirmations is a great tool to break old thinking habits.

Don't be surprised if life appears to get crazy. When you change the way you believe, the way you perceive the outer world must change as well. That is a universal law.

For example, if you use affirmations to strengthen your belief in prosperity, the ideas of lack and limitation must disappear. Financial challenges may come in order for you to exercise your faith in what you cannot yet see. This is really an opportunity to trust that your Eternal Identity is your Source, not the world you live in.

In the following story, Denise L shared with me that she had had a turbulent relationship with her mother since she was a small child. She could never do anything *right*. As an adult, Denise still carried the grief and shame of shattered emotions. While working as an accountant for a large medical facility, she was diagnosed with a tumor mass in her throat. (The throat chakra involves communication.) She had not talked to her mother in over a year. Surgery was scheduled to determine if the blockage was cancerous.

After much deliberation, Denise decided to call her mother to let her know about the surgery. From that single phone call prompted by a crisis, the healing between Denise and her mother began. Her intention was to recover and heal the relationship she had with her mother. At the time, Denise was using an affirmation to bolster her belief that "God's love heals all relationships." Sometimes we think *bad things are happening,* and they do happen! But as you move through the door of uncertainty, you may well open a door to heal a rift in your relationship with *that certain someone.*

Keep an open mind. The universe knows how to create changes. It doesn't always come through in a way that you have imagined.

You will learn to break the cycle of default thinking. As you launch into these affirmations, you will feel a shift in your energy. They make positive statements. Even if they seem foreign to you right now, I assure you that the neurotransmitters that relate to your brain as you guide it through this book will eventually manifest into better ways of thinking and feeling. In science, this is called neuroplasticity. What that basically means is that by using affirmations, you are establishing new habits which create new pathways in the brain, which will ultimately become your new way of thinking.

It's a start!

Imagine

All wisdom rising up within you is Divine by nature.

Affirmation

I am a tower of strength, power and confidence.

You are lined up to receive all words of Wisdom. Have faith in concluding that all Wisdom rising up within you is Divine by nature. It is available to you at any time of the day or night. Release past hurts. Forgive the transgressors that have crossed your path. Forgive yourself!

In her book, "May Cause Miracles," Gabrielle Bernstein says: "Forgiving the ego for having a particular negative thought is a very powerful tool. In the moment you forgive the thought, you're acknowledging that you are not your fear."

Although you may have experienced fear, regret and loneliness in the past, release these feelings and replace them with better feelings. Let go of the notion that you have been victimized. Bear witness to the truth. In the past, I allowed myself to wander into unsavory experiences that didn't turn out well.

From now on, I advise you to create your own reality and avoid some of the messes I made for myself. We all go through seas of despair, but if we allow ourselves to recover by being forgiving, a tower of strength, power and confidence will arise within you.

Influence resides in your relationship to the greater part of you— your Eternal Identity, the Higher Self that will always and only reveal to you every opportunity to find personal happiness. A safe place of holiness.

As you reach for knowledge, no harm can befall you. Invite this guidance. The more you practice tuning in to the knowledge that supports you, the better you will feel. And the better you feel, the happier you are. The happier you are, the more satisfied you will be. As you gather satisfying thoughts, you will be inspired by a feeling of control. As you regain control, you are restored to balance. In balance, you experience peace.

Imagine

Living your life from the inside out.

Affirmation

I release all fear and live in peace.

In the next chapter, we're going to look at the belief system and all the factors that continue to support that belief system. It's too big a job to change the entire network you have trained yourself to be throughout your life. Instead, say: *I am going to start changing the thoughts that put obstacles in my path right here, right now. I am going to stop self-sabotaging myself.* Use first person affirmations. It doesn't matter what you thought before, or for how long, or how many pressures you have been under to maintain limiting thoughts. Instead, activate thoughts that serve you being surrounded by abundance from the four Principles of: *Transformation, Change, Adaptability* and *Self-Realization.*

We will take a look at how to adapt your imagination to create value. When you imagine what you want, you feed energy to your dreams and goals. Allow yourself to feel what it would be like to already have what you want. Affirm the next step by bringing your body into alignment with your inner world. The outside world is your mirror and will reflect whatever it is you are holding within.

You can create nearly anything you desire today by simply tapping into the power of your imagination. I use affirmations to develop hope. I leave a trail in every chapter of this book. When you start to visualize something, you are in charge of the process. Deliberately direct your thoughts toward a positive outcome. Ask yourself, "Does this inspire faith?"

Here are a few examples of the way you might want to start with this exercise. Then you can put a name on words that inspire you and do so with conscious intention.

I am worthy.
I am wise.
I am blessed.
I am protected.
I am in the flow.
I am highly favored.
I am fearless.
I am accomplished.
I am respected.
I am revered.
I am smart.

Imagine

Shifting your focus from perceived
failures or inadequacies. Then directing
your focus toward your strengths.

Affirmation

*I allow myself to focus on my personal vision.
I have created a clear picture of what
I want my life to look like in the years ahead.
I use my imagination to support that picture with
written affirmations and positive thoughts.*

Chapter 2

The Value of Affirmations as Self-Care

SCAN ME

(or view my message on YouTube)
https://www.youtube.com/watch?v=yUodz8vEvjE

My dearly departed mother-in-law had a saying she frequently used whenever she made a flub. She would lift her hands in the air as if acknowledging her imperfections and say, "*Pobody's Nerfect!*" She might have really been on to something! Most of us strive for perfection in many ways, but we are not perfect. Everybody makes mistakes. We often say things others take offense to. If we are living our truth, it shouldn't make a difference whether anyone else thinks what we said was selfish or not, right or not.

The value of using this process isn't aimed at beating yourself up to solve the problem. Affirmations are used as self-care designed to get you to a better feeling place. As you build trust in this process, its value will show up as a suspension of negativity. Higher Consciousness will bring you to a place of relief. As you distract yourself by taking the focus off negative thoughts, you will experience solace. You can't *fix* anything if you are out of alignment with the perfection at your core.

People often confuse self-care with selfishness. This is not the case. In order to take care of others, you must first learn to take care of yourself. You are worthy of love, flaws and all. Like everyone, you have strengths and weaknesses. We are all works in progress. Affirmations are a self-help strategy used to promote self-confidence and belief in your own abilities. I encourage you to affirm yourself by whispering soft thoughts like the following:

All I can do is my best.
I've got what it takes.

I believe in my ability to succeed.

These simple statements help shift your focus away from perceived failures or inadequacies and direct your focus toward your strengths —those you already have and those you want to develop.

Affirmations of value help boost your self-esteem by reaffirming your worth. They get you back into the frequency of self-love, accepting who you are, understanding Divinity, and tapping into gratitude for self. Repeating affirmations at least once every day will rewrite your neuropathways and set you up for success in every area of your life. They add incremental value as you affirm the ideas and notions you focus on.

You get to write the script. Your brain has the ability to change and adapt to different circumstances throughout your life. Your mind offers clues that help you understand how affirmations work and how to use them in the most effective ways for you.

The brain actually doesn't know the difference between reality and imagination. This can be surprisingly useful, especially if you're creating a mental image of yourself doing something dangerous like hang-gliding off a cliff or scuba diving with sharks. It activates many of the same brain areas that experiencing these situations would. To love yourself is to know yourself. As you focus on what is going right in your experience, more of the same will flow. The evolutionary process is a simple one. It's easy to do, and also easy not do to.

We don't create with affirmations. We create by setting intentions with imaginary visualizations toward a scenario we would like to attain. By quieting your mind from negative chatter, you align with satisfaction. I call it the happiness factor. This allows what you are asking for, even if it isn't related to the declaration.

Affirmations aren't written as an exercise in creating what you want. It's more like aligning with what you've already created. It's never about effort. It's about allowing.

Affirmations are powerful because they get you on the other side of despair, anxiety, worry, and feeling defeated or deflated. As you learn from affirmative action, you magnify the solution. Affirmations, whether you write one or read one, add value to your life. Affirmations can be used as an aid to adapt to a more favorable mindset.

Conjure up an image for the purpose of creating a desired result. All visualization is simply mentally practicing an idea you have already asked for.

Look at an idea as a matter of fact before the physical evidence appears. Learn to pay more attention to the visualization of a finished product. Pay less attention to what your "reality" seems to be in the moment.

Using affirmations is not like taking a test. You're directly experimenting with yourself and your way of thinking. If things don't change as soon as you think they should, don't give up or quit! Don't look for the physical evidence and feel discouraged by the lack of proof of what you hoped to manifest. As long as you are feeling optimistic, you are in alignment with your desire. It's in the process of becoming. Find one thing about the process to be optimistic about and you will see everything else fall into place. It's like a domino effect.

You may feel dreamy or imaginative and want to mentally travel to faraway places like Bali or Hawaii or the Appalachian trail. Perhaps you're seeking more excitement in your life or are in a relaxed mood and simply want to enjoy a few minutes to daydream. Maybe you want to attract a lover, or a healthy business environment or a balanced body.

Creative visualization can be a powerful tool, whether you are trying to improve your circumstances or escape your daily routine. Close your eyes and envision the scene you wish to see in the future today, right now. An important aspect of visualization isn't only what you see, but how you feel, along with the emotion behind it. If you can allow yourself to feel the way you would if your vision were actually happening on a physical level, your experience will have an opportunity to materialize.

As a side note, when you dream in a sleep state, it's more important to pay attention to how the dream made you feel. All of us have said, "I had the weirdest dream last night!" Sometimes the strange dreams we have at night are hard to explain, but dreams can often parallel what's going on emotionally in our waking world.

Write about what you want and why you want it. The Universe will deliver the HOW.

> *"You have a unique set of precious values that can only be fulfilled by pursuing what drives you the most: your passions and dreams."*
> —Mike Dooly

You can use the power of creative affirmations by using your imagination. This magnifies beneficial circumstances and improves all aspects of your life.

Some years ago, I created a prosperity journal. I took one 8-1/2 x 11 piece of paper and taped it to my refrigerator. Begin right now. I promise, you will LOVE this practice!

I started keeping track of all the money that came into my life that I didn't earn. Call them gifts. I put the date and the year because I keep these lists from year to year. I remind myself of my good fortune. As you appreciate, you attract more things to appreciate!

Tape a dollar bill across the top of the page and write on it:

Thank you for all the money I have been given in my life!

Remember the small savings daily. Unexpected checks that come in the mail. A reduction in your electricity bill. Prescription drug savings (the difference between what the insurance paid and what comes out of your pocket). You can even list what you saved at the grocery store. On the end of every receipt, most stores are happy to tell you about your savings! The list goes on. Insurance refunds, tax relief, dental treatment, free lodging, tech support, trades, sale items, gifts, travel expenses, and so on. Do you have a friend who is a plumber willing to do you a favor? How about an electrician?

Keep track of the hours they volunteer and add all that to your list. A hundred dollars or more an hour adds up fast!

Your imagination is powerful. Your mind is capable of creating nearly anything you want while on planet earth! While manifestation may be a gradual process, visualizing and practicing what you want to create is the first step. When you imagine what you want, you feed energy to your dreams and goals.

At the end of the year, add your list! You will be shocked at how much money materializes out of thin air. In my case, at the time of writing this book, it's $16,810.63, and the year hasn't even ended yet!

Allow yourself to feel what it would be like to already have what you want. Baby steps bring you into alignment with your inner world. You can create nearly anything you desire today by simply tapping into the power of your imagination. Think of it! (I mean that quite literally!)

Imagine

Being okay with being imperfect.

Affirmation

I am worthy of Love, flaws and all.

In the next chapter, I encourage you to write a new story that will better serve you!

In review, we see that regular repetition of affirming statements about yourself can encourage your brain to take positive affirmations as fact. When you truly believe you can do something, your actions often follow.

As you give yourself permission to dream a new dream, you will realize that you are limitless. Every time you question yourself, every time you are afraid to fall, tap into your inner voice which will tell you the truth. You are worthy to receive anything you ask for. As mortals, we will never be totally fearless, but we can determine to replace fearful thoughts by releasing them. Purposefully write a new story that will better serve you. The thoughts you bring to mind are the first steps toward self-realization.

Thoughts become emotions, and sentiments are the guidance we need to be in control. Most people want to attract a soulmate, friends, a dream college, a more appealing physical appearance, financial stability, and peace of mind. There is an endless stream of well-being in all areas of life. Push away your doubts and follow your intuition. Enter a new adventure of gracious living toward yourself and everyone else in your natural environment, acquaintances, schoolmates, business associates and extended family. Create a ripple of positive thinking that will go out into the whole world!

As you talk about what you are passionate about, you will attract people who will hold a candle for your cause. They will take it into their hearts and carry a torch that will display a glowing light for all to enjoy. It will never be about the words you say, but how you make yourself and others feel, by the power of employing affirmative thoughts.

Nothing is impossible in this world, and you can demonstrate it over and over to yourself. Wake up every morning with an undefeatable determination to prove that to yourself over and over again.

If you can stir up the fire in just one person's heart to follow their dream, the mission for your purpose in life will complete itself. Invite your Eternal Identity to help you let go of your cares and seek the powerful Inner Presence of happiness, joy, peace and contentment.

Imagine

Allowing your Inner Hero
to be central to the decisions you make.

Affirmation

*I imagine how it feels to be inspired
by my Inner Hero.
My actions come from a truly enlightened space.*

Chapter 3

What's Your Story?

(or view my message on YouTube)
https://www.youtube.com/watch?v=9WFh0hpYCcU

Y our story matters and it's time for you to share it with the world. Share your story with at least one person today. Be brave and speak your truth.

Write your life story with a beginning, middle and end.

You were born into this physical environment in contrast. Contrast is both a noun and a verb. According to the dictionary, contrast as a noun means being strikingly different from its opposite. Think of the blue sky. We know that the sky is blue all the time. But when clouds roll in, you can't see the blue sky, yet cloudy and blue skies both exist at the same time. As a verb, contrast is the action of calling attention to notable differences. Let's use the example of right and wrong behaviors.

When you are born, you instinctively know what is true and good. However, there are lower energies that sometimes surround a little one through no fault of his or her own. It happens to all of us at one point or another as we grow up. Your parents did the best they knew how to do. In most cases, you were nurtured in childhood. But there are always unexpected emergencies, expenses, heartache and loss. There will be sunshine as well as darkness. The moon reflects light, even beyond the veil of clouds that cast dark shadows.

As you write your own life story, you will find that there is no benefit in pushing against the unwanted. Go with the flow of life! As you do, you will begin to notice a fine line has been created between your physical being and your inner being. This balance will have positive effects in all areas of your life.

Practice the abundance of all that is available to you, starting with the things in life that are free. Air, water, sunlight, beauty…The more you appreciate the things that are free, the more you will attract joy and happiness. Isn't happiness all we really ever want? There will be noticeable differences. You will feel better. You will lose any lethargy, sadness and despair. It's exciting to discover that when you know what you don't want, then you can change your focus so it will shine a light on what you do want.

There will be diversity as we have previously discussed. Children are aware of their divine connection. Most children find joy and wonder in watching butterflies, smelling rose bushes, seeing dragonflies, hummingbirds, cats and dogs. As children mature, they begin to ask themselves: "Who am I? What is holy or divine? Angels, guides, God? Inspiration, intuition, good? All the names for God?" If I were to sum up God's name in just one word, it would be an infinite *Supply*.

Even if "infinite supply" sounds mysterious, the very nature of God renders the wisdom of this world to be inadequate. Mystery does not mean mysterious or difficult to understand. It denotes a truth hidden in the Conscious mind (realm). Trust the sacred space between the small ego self and transition to living the supplied life – an abundant life. Meditate. Go to the place of surrender, so you can receive what is coming from a higher vibration which is much more powerful than logic.

Guides and wonders, revelations, angels, nature helpers, people, places, experiences, synchronicities, passages, urgings, and passion will appear in your conscience. Nurture these thoughts and you will see them manifest by the same law that keeps the planets in perfect synchronicity to other planets. Are you ready to step onto the path of self-realization?

In the following paragraphs, I hope to make a parallel between the pages in a book and the book of life in real time.

Imagine that you are holding a book in the palms of your hands. You have chosen this book and eagerly anticipate opening it up to the first page. You were attracted by the cover. You read the inside of the book jacket. You were inspired to make the purchase. You are familiar with the author.

The ethereal realm suggests that before you came to earth from the eternal state of being, you were given a glimpse of what would be available to you during your life in physical form. If you were to compare your life to that of an open book, you might agree that only God knows the time and space you were delivered onto the planet.

In Luke Chapter 7 in the New Living translation of the Bible, it is stated, "And the very hairs on your head are numbered." This would indicate that there is a plan for your life before you are even born.

You make careful preparations for opening to the first page of the book. Perhaps you will make a cup of tea, or light a fire in the fireplace or ignite the flame on the wick of a scented candle. You grab a couch pillow and a comfortable cotton throw from the back of the sofa. You have plenty of light to illuminate the pages. You open the book, and begin to read the introduction.

Like a book, the segments of your life are in chronological order. You savor chapter one. (Most babies are celebrated.) You are the opening statement. You have been looking forward to this moment so you can explore the delicacies of the book called Life. You are in high expectation and settle in for a good read.

Your life is like a novel. The chapters are laid out carefully. Each chapter has its own title and the number of events it represents. It plays out incrementally. You develop many bodies from birth to old age. You shed and stretch your skin, grow your organs, experience youth, vigor and eventually old age.

Each good story has a beginning, middle and end. In the beginning, the story often reads like an expression of hope. The characters seem to think they know what they want. You get a clear vision of what's happening. You have a certain expectation of what the book is about. You turn the page and become part of the story. By chapter three, you are completely engaged. But wait...you begin to see some angst developing.

Just like life itself, what you were anticipating can take an unexpected twist. An uncanny development is clouding your view. Worked up, you get up and take a break from reading, pondering the outcome, feeling unsettled, worried. This is not the story you created in your mind. What went wrong?

Enter contrast.

In the back of your mind, you hope the author will bring you to some kind of resolution. Surely there will be a happy ending? After all, you didn't expect to enter into a story that would be disappointing at the conclusion.

Life has many twists and turns. There are often forks in the road. Which choice to make? You may stand in indecision, wondering which option you should take. There are others to consider. The plot thickens. You could spend days, months and even years sitting on the fence of indecision.

You stop reading and wander around the house again. Check your email, go to the potty, refresh your tea, and eat a cookie (even though you know you shouldn't). But, what the heck? You need something to take the edge off. You have dedicated this time and space to reading. You are committed to finishing the book. You're not in a hurry exactly, but you're eager to see the way the story plays out.

In your own life, sooner or later you will have to let go of the analysis and self-doubt that you have been holding onto. There is no way you can be certain about the results of your choices. During your lifetime, you will be called upon to consider which direction resonates with you the most and then take action. Taking action will shatter fragmented and confused energies so you can bring new structure to your plans and your life.

You return to your safe haven. You've had your break from reading. You jump in again with both feet, eyes wide open. You take a deep breath and begin again. Chapter eight. Trouble is on the horizon. Will the heroine get the help she needs? Will search and rescue arrive on time? The unknown is frightening! In the middle of the passages, safety seems unsure. Which road should you take? You look for clarity and assurance. You may not have known what to do in the past, but your Inner Hero has been trying to guide you all along.

Just like the author of a good story, you have the option to create your life the way *you* want *your* story to unfold. Open up to the potential of this dash between birth and death. Then let yourself move forward with purpose, exercising your personal power. Will you rely on outside forces to determine your destiny? Or will you reach within the confines of Higher Consciousness for certain answers? Release fear and move forward with courage and trust. You will be glad you did!

Adopt the philosophy of your own well-being. Putting yourself first is not being selfish. It's the greatest gift you can give to yourself because only you can live your life. No one else can do it for you.

Spirit delights when you come to the table to feast on the blessings that are offered to you. It is in the quiet of a motionless mind that your Eternal Identity will speak. Invite it. Be assured that there is no part of that still small voice that will interfere with your free will to choose.

Do you have an open mind? The flow from everlasting light is always available to you. Only you have the power to write your own story. Your body is the vessel that carries your spirit. The spirit is the all-knowing Higher Self, the energy, the voice, the value of reckoning. It is within your Eternal Identity that all answers to the questions on any subject remain to be revealed at your request. For every woe, there is a blessing. For those who mourn, there will be a comforter. If a void is created, there will be something else to fill it.

It is when you are in alignment with this Inner Being that you begin to awaken. Your desire was so strong to experience life that some of you forfeited a comfortable childhood. And yet you do recover as you rediscover your inherent strengths. You are a person with the capacity to revive your inner child. You can play out the life you want to live. We have come to the physical realm to learn from experience. You can find freedom from the limitations, fears, feelings of unworthiness and other traits you might have grown up around. Learn to adopt your own philosophy of well-being as you unlearn negative thoughts and behaviors.

Your Eternal Identity will shed light on any and all circumstances, no matter how dark they may seem. Higher Consciousness only sees the light. As you ask, your Inner Hero will show you the glow. If you could see who walks before you, behind you, beside you, within you, you would never be afraid again.

Your Eternal Identity knows that there is really no end to the story. Only the end of *this* story. When you close the final chapter of this book called Life, other adventures will present themselves. A new plot, a different twist, a happy ending, or not…You, the author, have the capacity to write each page. Build on present thought, based on past experience. Launch towards future endeavors with an outward and ongoing assurance that there is always a means to an end.

Life is made up of chapters. Some are pleasing, some are intolerable, but they all make up the story of your life. Each day is a clean slate. How will you write your future? Does it have a happy ending? Life unfolds in direct proportion to what you attract to it. Each moment unfolds from the choices you make today. You live and you learn. Unlike the novel, there never really is an ending.

How many books are in you? There's never a final draft. The joy is in the unfolding. The invitation to come and play remains infinite, alluring, inspired by passion, evolutionary, complete and incomplete, all at the same time.

Imagine yourself gaining the courage to be all that you can be. Imagine how it feels to be courageous. Harness the power of your mind and come to the place of harmony. Embrace the changes that are necessary to thrive and grow.

You chose the environment you were born into for the contrast and the variety you knew would be laid out before you. Get excited about opportunities that present themselves to you in an environment of change. There are many options to choose from and challenges provide an opportunity to create lasting change and transformation.

Most of our priorities include safety and security. You feel a lot of this most of the time. But you also want to be inspired by adventure so that your senses may be stirred to quick decisions. You want to add spontaneous excitement and anticipation to the expedition that lies dormant in the confines of your mind. Awaken the sleeping giant within!

How will you know you have lived at all if you do not test the courage to be all you can be? You are your own storyteller. You are the victim. You are the villain. You are the hero. You are the victor. You are all the things you see as possible in this lifetime. Built moment upon moment, making up you. Do not squander one ounce of the protection that is the Higher Self, the energy, the all of you. You are the author of all you do. It only can begin…have a middle and an end…with you.

Life is a great teacher. Let's take a look at how we can overcome adversity when we never asked for it in the first place! In the next chapter, we are challenged to find any good in several situations, but the stance you take cannot be dependent on another's behavior. Sometimes it's better to be kind, quiet or both!

There will be moments when you encounter a person who behaves rudely toward you or someone else in their midst. It might help to remember that you don't know what difficulties someone might be going through. They may be feeling unwell, or overburdened. They may have just lost a loved one, or be in the midst of a divorce. Some may have been fired from their job, feel desperate and are at a turning point in their life. Perhaps they feel unloved themselves. People who are hurting themselves often hurt other people. Your gratitude and kindness might be the most wonderful thing that happens to them that day.

Imagine

I bring clarity and wisdom to the world.
I find my voice and let my light shine.

Affirmation

I surround myself with serenity in silence,
and perceive the wisdom of my Eternal Identity.

Chapter 4

Your Constant Companion and Your Well-Being

(or view my message on YouTube)
https://www.youtube.com/watch?v=sUJKJgvqAwk

I wake up to the truth of my eternal wisdom, talents and abilities and take the risk of believing in myself.

Every ego has a spiritual connection.

What many people call God is Consciousness that is expanding. The small ego is defined as a person's personality, esteem or self-importance. It's not easy to see the big picture from a physical perspective until you come to the realization of insight through personal experience. Life is a great teacher.

People are accustomed to using the way they feel to determine the outcome of their actions. If you're angry, defeated, discouraged, upset or depressed, you may miss or ignore the intuitive part of your being.

Those in society who are not aligned with their Constant Companion often make decisions driven by a lack of clarity. Indecision, self-appointed shame, relationship issues and similar interactions often suffer as a result.

Your ego is often out of balance with your spirit. Every person born on earth has a soul, an emotional guide that leads, suggests, helps, and protects. This is what I continue to call your Eternal Identity, Higher Consciousness, Infinite Intelligence, Creator, the Divine, Inner Hero, and the Supply throughout this book. It is all-knowing, pure Love and energy directly related to you. However, when we solely rely on the guidance of our small ego, we sometimes falter.

The same impulse that inspires appreciation for you to enjoy the scent of a flower, or a feeling of love for an animal or a child, can also wreak havoc when spinning out of control. Higher Consciousness represents all good compared to the sharp contrast the ego offers.

Let me explain what I mean by "sharp contrast."

Higher Consciousness represents all good. The ego wants and feels a need to be validated. There will be a tug of war inside you when the ego is challenged. People have opinions and they most often will fight for what they consider to be "the right perspective." People will then try to justify why their behavior has value. If their way of thinking is interpreted as being out of alignment with what others believe, then they get defensive and feel as if they're being attacked.

There are a lot of "high drama" people in the world who seem to thrive in toxic conditions. Unfortunately, that's just the way it is. When your ego is out of balance with your Inner Hero, aggressive behaviors often result, as is the case in the following story.

Several days ago, I was the unfortunate witness of someone whose ego was clearly out of balance. Although this is not the first time I have seen this, I was deeply disturbed by the experience.

I was in a booth at a fast food restaurant enjoying a cup of coffee while my car was being serviced. A woman came in with two unkempt kids, to my best guess around the ages of four and six. The mother was in the midst of settling her children in a booth.

For whatever reason, she was clearly worked up and unnerved. She shuffled her bags while complaining to herself, naturally capturing my attention. She was agitated, angry and even unkempt herself.

As unsettled as it made me feel, I tried to mind my own business. The woman noticed that her two children were ignoring her complaints. Without warning, the woman slapped her little girl. The child was disheveled and fell off the bench, further infuriating her mother. "Get up!" she screeched.

The child whimpered. As I watched, fear set into the little girl's sweet sensitive spirit. She began to cry. Her brother gaped, and sat all the way back into his seat, trying to be invisible. He was powerless, but didn't dare take his eyes off his mother.

He monitored her every move. I could almost hear his thoughts. Tears streamed down the face of the little girl with the untidy hair and soiled face as she cowered under the table. At this point, it was all I could do not to interfere. Instead of sending the woman love, I stared at her in contempt.

The woman realized she had caused a stir. She caught me staring at her. She frowned and returned my gaze with piercing brown eyes.

Daring me to interfere, she threw her hands in the air. Without speaking, she implied, "What are you looking at?!"

With every fiber of my being, I wanted to prevent further danger to the children and possibly risk injury myself. I'm certain you can understand how I felt!

As unsettling as an incident like this might be, you cannot ever change the conduct of another person.

Sad as it is, this is an example of how little control we have over the behavior of someone who is out of alignment.

While all of us are subject to bad days, if you're in alignment with your core values, such as patience, grace, goodwill, honesty and integrity, you have a better chance of catching yourself in undesirable behaviors and stopping them in their tracks.

All of us suffer from blows to our egos that we don't expect. Someone is rude. You walk into a room where coworkers are gossiping about you. You know this because as soon as you walk in, their conversation abruptly stops.

Everyone feels assaulted from time to time. As a result of our previous conditioning, our identity (ego) becomes threatened. This means the ego fears for its safety and protection. Drama is often the result.

Let's take a look at what we *can* do to support ourselves and return to balance whenever we get out of whack.

Letting go of the angst of wrongdoing requires a deep trust in your Eternal Identity. We catch glimpses of this Higher Self when we feel elation, joy, bliss, empowerment, stability, resonance, and ecstasy, all of which are the opposites of feeling angst.

You are responsible for lining up with your Spiritual Guide. As you own a belief and practice it, you will be provided an opportunity to adopt a new philosophy, one that serves you and which will ultimately serve all those around you. This practice of thought will resonate so deeply within you that there will be no other way in which you will want to live.

Right and wrong choices speak volumes to fellow travelers on this path of earthly life. Others close to you will pay attention to your actions, whether consciously or subconsciously. Some could look at the way you live and be in awe, wondering for themselves, "How does she do it?"

Others might be angry at you for not conforming to the standards they have long held for you. Learn to soar higher. As you practice making conscious decisions that are in alignment with your highest and best self, you will no longer wish to live life the way you did in the past. That said, in the midst of your inner circle, there could still be misunderstandings. That's because not everyone is aligned with their true self at the same time. Everyone's path in life is different and people grow and evolve at their own pace.

There is nothing you can do or say about it. However, it could be that your own altered behavior might make a difference in those around you. In other words, *change*. Life experience is a great task master. Not everyone will be ready to take that first step on their path to *self-realization*. But you can apply your influence by becoming a positive role model.

Choose to experience excitement, anticipation and joy. Test your expression as being a spirit having a human experience. Know there will be trials and tribulations. There will always be people you don't agree with and those who will not agree with you.

You always have an Inner Hero, one who has your best interests at heart, the soul center of your well-being. It's the Consciousness that keeps your feet from stumbling. Intuitive eyes that recognize and avert danger. The angel with his abiding help to cross the many bridges you must traverse to get to the other side. You are your own hero. You came in from Source and you have an abundance of inner resources. Allow yourself to receive, and enjoy.

Imagine

Partnering with your Inner Hero
who has your best interests at heart.

Affirmation

*I travel, not on my own,
but with the Constant Companion
who came with me at birth.*

In the next chapter, I will take you on a tour of what your life might look like as you decide your own fate. Within you today lives the knowledge that you are the creator of your own life experience.

You build your future by living in the present. All anybody has is this moment, right now. The past is history and the future is unknown. Freedom exists in taking responsibility to influence your own life. You are the only one who can govern your fate.

The whole universe fits together for the perfection of the plans you decide to carry out or not. Motion forward is inevitable, but you are not here to compete with your own life experience. You are here to enjoy the unfolding of every single day in line with the destiny only *you* can inspire.

Imagine

Being the keeper of your present moments.

Affirmation

*As I direct my destiny, the mists of the future
will turn into brilliant clarity.*

Chapter 5

An Appointment
With Your Destiny

SCAN ME

(or view my message on YouTube)
https://www.youtube.com/watch?v=Z1lOCuEDmrE

Consider all your options and then adopt an action plan toward change. This is your time for a new beginning of Divine inspiration and personal growth.

Is your future fixed?

At its core, the notion of destiny refers to the idea that there are predetermined events in your life. But destiny is a concept that you have the power to shape and change. All of us at one time have asked the question, "What is my destiny?" Most of us are curious about what will happen to us in the future.

Are you destined to meet Mr. Right, or Ms. Wrong? Do you have any control over your destiny or is it predetermined by an unknown lifeforce? Why were you born into a particular family? Is there a hidden power that will control what will happen in the future?

Destiny is sometimes referred to as fate. Fate alludes to a predetermined course of someone's life. According to the dictionary, fate as a noun refers to the development of events beyond a person's control. Fate is regarded as determined by a supernatural power.

Destiny emphasizes the impression of an unalterable course of events. It's an elusive philosophical concept that our fate or destiny is fixed. To a degree, it is.

Each one of us gains a theoretical basis of a particular branch of knowledge as a result of how far we ourselves have grown and evolved in this life. Every theory or attitude is developed further as you agree with guiding principles that resonate with you and not someone else. You are the authority in and of your own life.

Your spiritual destiny is eternal. You came into the world with it, and it never leaves you. It's the rebirth of your soul in your body.

As you have learned so far, you make thousands of choices every day. As you choose, you create with your free will. Life unfolds through actions. Your life evolves and changes with every moment. Transformation is inevitable. Destiny implies that something has already been decided. If that's true, then what would be left to discover?

If it is your destiny, the universe will make sure you find it. Granted, there is order in the universe, but serendipitous developments happen all the time. You are always in the right place at the right time.

Your destiny will choose you as demonstrated in the following story. Self-realization may not happen overnight. It can, but most often our predetermined thought patterns need time to germinate. Like a seed planted in the ground, growth breaks through the topsoil and expands outward.

Imagine

This is a time for a new beginning of
Divine Inspiration and personal growth.

Affirmation

I am the authority in and of my own life.

Maggie and Cyril met as young adults while at the Lackland Air Force Academy in Texas. It is currently known as Joint Base San Antonio. Cyril was from New York, and Maggie was from Alabama. Both parties were far from their original homes.

They found their friendship deepening in the course of six weeks of continuing education. The problem was that Cyril was already betrothed to another woman back home. His girlfriend was devoted to him and they had a long-standing relationship. There was a promise of building a life together, a promise that Cyril would not break. As a result, he did not act on the pull of his heart towards Maggie.

Life went on. Cyril married and had several children. Maggie had some long-term relationships, but never married. She was content with her small sturdy beagle, her beloved companion, and went on with her life.

Fast forward forty years later.

Both Cyril and Maggie had retired. Cyril's wife had transitioned five years earlier. Lonely, Cyril looked for and found Maggie via Facebook. Cyril called Maggie and they had a long and exuberant conversation. They seemed to pick up right where they had left off decades before.

The next week, Cyril had a bouquet of flowers in his hand when he rang Maggie's doorbell. Finally, he was free to act on the opportunity to build a solid relationship with Maggie, no strings attached.

Why not take a chance? Lean in the direction your soul prompts you to take. You will be moved toward what it is you are drawn to. You will gravitate towards it. You will know you are on track when it feels right. Your destiny activates intuition.

It's your Inner Being agreeing with the direction you take towards your next step. You can feel the alignment with broader evidence. You will know when you are off track because your "gut" tells you that something is "off." Your destiny is coming into harmony with who you really are.

Your decision to move forward will propel you in the direction of great rewards. Destiny cannot be cast in stone. The past will not catapult you into the future. Your future evolves as a result of the decisions you make today.

Destiny is not literal. Destiny is evolution towards happiness. Your destiny will call you to it moment by moment.

You have an appointment with destiny. It is your particular function to merge with the Divine. As you do, you will tap into infinite wisdom and understanding.

If your destiny (or fate) were already discovered or decided, you wouldn't have been born into the world to explore. It would leave out the whole experience of your own creation. Listen to the message Spirit delivers, receive it, and act on it. Your rebirth draws near.

You will be protected by the presence of angels. Be open to receive in abundant measure. Spiritual strength and life are yours as you claim them, unless you decide to give these powers away. What you *think* is acceptable and possible can and *will* become true for you.

It is wise to let go of all "error words" so that you can be an instrument of guidance and direction. Error words are what some call "old tapes" or old programming running through your mind. These govern your self-talk, the statements you say to yourself either in your mind or actually out loud. These can be statements such as, "I can't ever do anything right. I'm no good. I don't deserve to have nice things. I've always been unlovable." Any similar thoughts are not the truth about who you really are.

Seek peace and presence within the confines of your mind and heart. They are always there, offering to guide and direct you. Pay attention and listen. Intuit the area of your mind that is receptive. Release all resistance, both past and present.

Without resistance, you can begin to hear with clarity and confidence. Do you wish to capture the slightest message from your beneficent guide, your Eternal Identity? Human intellect can merge with the Divine. It will feel right. It's your Inner Being agreeing with the direction you choose as you take your next steps.

You are the river of life. Higher Consciousness flows into your soul, keeping you eternally young. Let all disharmonies pass into nothingness. You are destined to be eternally free.

Imagine

Being an open channel through which
the river of life may flow.

Affirmation

*The inspiration of my Eternal Identity
fills me with grace.*

Be conscious of the Oneness of all. Be showered by the Omnipresence who will sustain you and uphold you. The inspiration of your Eternal Identity fills you. Rest in the presence of peace and relax. Let the waters of life wash over you.

Agree with the cleansing and purifying process taking place in you as your body is aligned with the Divine Mind. Your Eternal Identity is the strength of your heart. Your flesh rests in this hope.

As often as you can, adopt thoughts of joy, appreciation, satisfaction, abundance, clarity, decision, grace, anticipation, and humility. None of these emotions are man-made. Find alignment with your Source first, and all the things that you want will be added to your experience. Trust that, as you believe it, you will see it. Leave doubt at the door!

Doubt comes in many forms, and does not unlock the door to your happiness. Guard against letting doubt in. Try to remember that worry is creating a story about what you *don't* want. It is uncomfortable to dwell on feelings of uncertainty, worry and anxiety. Those feelings interrupt the flow of life and create chaos. Listen to the silence, in appreciation and gratitude and, in it, you will find your voice.

Life presses onward in an unstoppable drive for the evolution of human awareness and expansion. In the next chapter, we will explore the many benefits of growing into your Inner Avatar.

We will also see that sometimes we allow ourselves to go towards the loudest noise. Televisions blare, the telephone rings, elements of social media and electronics interfere with a calm sense of clarity.

Kids get sick, business propositions fail. You get cut off in traffic, accidents happen. Not so good!

I hope you will be more careful than I was earlier in my life at truly paying attention. The direction of the thoughts you do *not* deliberately choose can be damaging! This is illustrated in the stories presented in the next chapter.

Imagine

The purpose of your life is to expand
in joy as a human being.

Affirmation

I contemplate much broader horizons.
I expand my global network.
I have unlimited resources available to me.
I dream BIG!

Chapter 6

Expanding Into
Your Inner Avatar

(or view my message on YouTube)
https://www.youtube.com/watch?v=NVMe6YMWNTE

Take time to focus with your Inner Avatar. Expansion will then have an avenue to take hold. In this chapter, Avatar is defined as an incarnate, divine teacher. This is another name for Higher Consciousness, the part of you that expands into something greater than yourself.

When your desires are really strong, that goes a long way toward triumph. Your desires will follow the path of least resistance and create avenues for Spirit to speak with you, guide and direct you. Give more attention to things that happen in your experience. You may want to pause and reflect on your thoughts and feelings before you move ahead.

You are constantly being guided to a deeper, more practical understanding of expansion. There is depth and breadth in the vast network affecting the steps you are guided to take. Through your everyday life, it is natural to expect well- being. Why do we resist?

The consequence of life is expansion, and the purpose of life is happiness. Evolution revolves around an ongoing relationship with your Inner Avatar, your incarnate, divine teacher. When you don't line up, things can go haywire in a hurry as demonstrated by the following stories.

The morning I was to get my annual physical started like many other mornings. I had done my journaling of appreciation before leaving the house. Once I got into my car, I said a prayer of protection and down the freeway I went.

Since I had moved to a new location, I met with a new doctor. The exam went fine. At the end of my physical, the young doctor who was attending to me said, "Now, don't fall!" I was startled. I consider myself to be in good shape. I swim daily to keep my joints loose. I didn't see any reason for him to say something to me like that, but I took it into my subconscious where it remained unchecked.

Later that afternoon, I was in a strange garage. I was doing a favor for a neighbor who asked me to check the mileage on a parked car in their absence. As a result of a remodel, the garage was filled with boxes of tile. They were about the same height as that of the seat on the open van's door.

The request completed, I stepped back away from the car door to close it. Can you guess what happened? Yes! I fell backwards over the tile boxes and landed on the back of my neck! Fortunately, I was unharmed. Clumsy me, I mused, reminding myself to be more careful.

Not two weeks later, I was having a conversation with my granddaughter over a basket of fish and chips.

"Do you remember when you were very young and you got your fingers slammed in the car door?" I asked, cringing.

"No, Grandma," she replied.

"Well, that's good!" I exclaimed. "I was hoping you would not remember. I don't even know why I brought it up."

Soon after, the family got into the twelve passenger van my son uses to transport his six kids. Guess what? I got my fingers caught in the door. Oh my gosh, I thought to myself after the entire drama was over. I attracted this accident as a result of my conversation with my granddaughter shortly before it happened.

Do you see the parallels between my fall and the smashed finger? Can you now see that the words you say to others can have an impact on them? That's why our words are so important, not just the things we tell ourselves, but also the things we say to others in our lives.

All things that happen in your experience come because you attract them with your thoughts. You get what you think about, whether you want to or not! None of us can guard our thoughts all the time. There are too many worldly distractions. However, paying attention to small nudges from your Inner Avatar can give you an edge. From now on, I am paying closer attention!

Deliberately nurture the inner teachings that are available to you.

You are wise to seek counsel from the Source. It is good to deliberately nurture the teachings that are available. They will provide a sense of clarity. You discover concepts whereby you can avoid unwanted circumstances by paying attention.

You will find that you are never scolded for seeking counsel. Your Inner Avatar is your best friend. You could not find a better relationship than that with your intimate, Eternal Identity.

Nothing can go wrong in this relationship. It is unlike those responses you get from your fellow human beings. As you tend to your relationship with your Eternal Identity, all other relationships with any other person, place or thing will be good. This is a big payday.

Your Inner Avatar is expanding as a result of what you think about. You are a reflection mirroring that expansion. Can you agree that there is no greater relationship that you can have but the one with yourself? It is certainly the only relationship you have control over.

Every person has their own opinion as to what they think and how they act. If you put ten people in a room and ask them the same question, they will come up with ten different answers. This is why looking to others for confirmation or validation is not dependable. It only strokes your ego.

Your ego is constantly on the lookout to feel significant and adored. The purpose of your small ego is for it to survive. It will constantly send you thoughts to preserve its existence. Just remember that you are more than your small ego. You are your Eternal Identity.

As you nurture your relationship with your Inner Avatar, you will have an influence on those you come into contact with without saying a word. It's osmosis!

Caring for your relationship with your Inner Hero, your internal teacher and guide, will gradually increase the process of assimilation of ideas and knowledge. It takes the cycle of life to a new place of understanding. You are a non-physical consciousness walking around in a human body. How wonderful this realization truly is!

You explore and expand, and that Source within you becomes the immediate and ongoing equivalent of that expansion. Preferences of inspiration to act upon certain premises are born as a result of your relationship with your Inner Being. The biggest proof of all? It shows on your face! You become radiant and literally full of light!

You are consistently being guided on the eternal journey by this light. It is an inherent part of you. A part invited by the consensus of your own free will. The human part of you that always gets to choose the direction of your thoughts. Spirit will only take you as far as you are ready and willing to go. Your work is to become a match to your Avatar.

As you nurture and care for your relationship with your Inner Being, you begin to trust the *evidence* without feeling a dependency. The proof will show up as an expression of what you affirm. Here's an example.

Years ago, I started to keep what I call my God Box. I chose a beautiful cardboard box purchased from Michael's arts and craft store. I set some time aside on a few weekends with a pile of magazines to cut items from and then started to build my dreams. I cut out pictures of happy relationships between friends. I cut out objects that I wanted to attract into my life, such as new appliances and so on.

I cut out a picture of a beautiful little girl and wrote the date on the back of the picture with a note in my own handwriting that said, *"If I were to have a granddaughter, I would like her to look just like this little girl."* Then I pushed the God Box to the back of my bedroom closet.

When I retrieved the box one year later, I found I had attracted more than a few of the items I had been looking forward to. It's amazing to me what happened! A lot more things came my way as well. New kitchen appliances, a hot tub, a kitten!

Four years into this process, my first-born granddaughter blessed us with her presence. Five years after that, I looked at the picture of the little girl I had originally dreamed of. They looked so much alike!

By applying this exercise, you will find that your grandest desires can and will come to pass. Remember that you must clearly communicate your desires to your ever-present Inner Avatar.

It will always be a two-way communication, even if sometimes you aren't the best listener. Don't worry. The solution to any problem will present itself again in a way you can relate to, understand and implement. The key is to pay attention and then take the action steps.

The energy stream that is you will always benefit the most by your alignment with it. Align with this energy or not.

Imagine

Being joined together in a never-ending circle of love
that leads to expansion.

Affirmation

I meditate on the side of the light,
keeping my eyes ever turned toward beauty and purity.

It's your choice to apply your free will at all times.

Let your Inner Avatar guide you and feed you. A vision of your perfection takes form in your outer world. Soon you will reflect the power and clarity that is your Divine inheritance. Trust utterly that you are an heir to all that is good. Source energy is always with you, giving you courage and strength.

You have a right side to your wrong. You have a friend, not a foe. Your relationship is secure. Your love is assured. Take the higher road, knowing you will be led to green pastures, watered by the springs of well-being.

You have a Constant Companion who is with you, closer than your every breath. You walk, talk, listen, and speak. You are supplied with an ever-present, supportive, caring, and trusting comrade, co-creators in the process of living your life. Together, you are the heads and tales sides of a coin. You are joined together in a circle of never-ending love and expansion, the active side of infinity here on planet earth.

It's alignment that draws manifestations, not you having to figure out what your next step is going to be. At the beginning of a new year, most of us make New Year's resolutions. At one time early in my career, I wrote pages and pages of these resolutions! We sometimes get carried away by making lofty goals. In the next chapter, I'll present a formula geared toward creating success in any endeavor.

It takes practice. It's the tone of your thoughts (pure positive emotion) that lets success in. Alignment eradicates doubt before doubt can take a foothold. Allow yourself to feel what it would be like to already have what you want. The world is your mirror and will reflect whatever dreams you are holding. You can create nearly anything you desire today by simply tapping into the power of your own imagination.

Imagine

Allowing yourself to quiet your mind and listen.
Being aligned with your deepest desires.

Affirmation

I am calm, peaceful and untroubled.

Chapter 7

The Art of Alignment
with a Quiet Mind

SCAN ME

(or view my message on YouTube)
https://www.youtube.com/watch?v=SHcd2tpSV7U

Y ou are the one you have been waiting for.

Do you sometimes find yourself on a path that leads to a fork in the road, not knowing which way to turn? Do you wish for guidance? By now, you have learned to turn inward. The answers will come.

The more practice you apply by going within, the greater you will trust the process. You will often be influenced by outside sources. This happens to everyone just because of the nature of our interactions with each other. We are relational beings. We often seek approval and we all want to feel loved, appreciated, and accepted for who we are.

Look less outside yourself for teachers and guides. The more you turn inward, the more you become your own muse. You attract what you think about into your existence. It becomes inevitable. You carry within yourself every bit of knowledge you need to make progress on your path to *self-realization*.

There is no hide and seek. Everything you need to know comes from the joy you feel when you line up with the aspect of Higher Consciousness that lives inside you. Your flesh and your spirit are not separate at any point you are alive while in this physical body.

You take yourself everywhere you go. There is no need to travel to find peace. The best instructors don't have the ability to point out answers you already inherently possess.

Recently, I saw a billboard advertising a local community college that read, *"We teach students how to think, not what to think."* I love that! You alone hold the answers for a quiet mind of happiness. Ultimately, you are the one you have been waiting for.

The people you might describe as having exceptional abilities are usually those who have practiced the art of alignment with a quiet mind. Let's take a look.

Professionals such as artists, sculptors, business people, musicians, bricklayers, teachers and other occupations who are passionate about what they do are using their creative imagination to produce their work.

They have come to a comfortable agreement with and understanding of who they really are. They pay attention to nudges and act responsibly. The only brilliance or clarity they claim is the intuitiveness they glean from listening to and following their inner guidance. People call it by different names, but it's the same awareness that resides inside each of us.

Leonardo DaVinci, painter of one of the most famous paintings on the planet, the Mona Lisa, has been quoted as saying, "If the spirit is not present, there is no art."

Seek alignment with your Inner Hero. This is where all the practicing comes in. Apply the art of alignment with a quiet mind. It gets easier and you start noticing more deeply as your awareness gets used to paying attention and then following through with whatever nudges you receive. These nudges don't always "hit you over the head." That's why you have to be quiet enough to be still and listen.

People are always looking for role models, mentors, teachers, ethereal entities and angels to guide them on their path. There is nothing wrong with this. I do it myself as I ask my guides to reveal themselves. However, it's important to realize that, in the absence of such a figure, you can very safely rely upon yourself, your Inner Hero.

Imagine

Practicing patience.
Spirit will reveal to you what it is you need to
know, sometimes in small increments.

Affirmation

I thank Consciousness for being part of me.
I appreciate the opportunity to get to know myself
better as I purposely practice having a quiet mind.

I love following a treasure map! There is the element of discovery along the way. There are riddles to be solved. There's a sense of adventure! Look at the art of alignment as a very valuable navigation system following the map of receiving your inner guidance.

As you learn and grow fond of using this tool towards *transformation*, you will find precious metals, gems and demonstrations of its power. You will attract relationships that sparkle like diamonds, even with people you might never have met otherwise.

Put one foot in front of the other on the path towards fulfillment. Life continues to be a surprise. Expect the best from people who advise you along the way, but trust yourself. Guides and guardian angels introduce you to synchronicities that inspire the larger part of who you are.

Remember that the decision to practice the art of alignment lies within you and you alone. Be assured that other-worldly entities always want the best for you. When invited, they will point you in the right direction. Your guides will never coerce or assert their influence on you. They are spiritual helpers only, but will never make decisions for you. That's where your free will comes into play.

Appreciate the teachers that you have learned from over the years, the men and women who have written volumes of great wisdom. You are a compilation of everything you have taken into your mind. Make a personal practice of all you have learned along the way.

Decide that you like being a "work in progress." Continue to believe you are highly favored and blessed. Less harm can come to you as you embrace this mindset. As you improve your skills, you will boost your confidence and replace self-doubt. You will learn to trust your inner compass.

By now, you have come to a comfortable agreement with these concepts. Negativity will bounce off of you more regularly. Take each step, day by day, moment by moment. You will feel resonance in your body, and you will know what is sure and right and true for you.

Every step on your path is meaningful. Even a step that seems to take you backwards is a motion forward. It feels like good sense for you to move to the next level.

In addition, an intense growth spurt requires that you rest for a time in order to fully integrate the new energies that have been liberated by your hard work. When you feel you aren't making progress in your internal growth, encourage yourself to take a moment to rest. Whatever it is you are feeling anxious about (it's usually pretty close to home), let it go!

Meditate more, feed yourself well, and get extra sleep. Before you know it, you will be eager to work toward the next level of your development. This rest will make sense as something we all need in order to continue as you cultivate introspection and *self-realization*.

Once the sun rises, it doesn't go backwards. Instead, it follows its path around the globe. It may appear to stand still for a moment in time, or to move more slowly at some point or another, but it is always steadily moving forward on its path.

It's the same with us. Once you have moved through an experience that has the potential to change your life, you can never really go back. You may be resting or revisiting issues that seem old, and it's natural to feel stuck, but, in truth, you are taking the next important steps.

The following chapter will provide examples of why any attachment to outcome is a great obstacle. We can never truly see or know the bigger picture, which is why practicing non-attachment is so important.

We commonly perceive others to be an extension of ourselves. We imagine that we know what's best for others, but people have their own ideas. Surprise!

By the same token, other people often put pressure on us to perform like they want us to. A great paradox arises around the issue of attachment. Despite what we feel is sound reasoning, it's absurd to believe that we have earned the right to step into someone else's shoes. You can never see life from behind someone else's eyes.

Is it fair to demand others to conform to our way of thinking because we're attached to a particular idea or outcome? I wouldn't want anyone making those decisions for me, would you? It is preposterous for us to expect someone to conduct themselves in a manner by which we command their actions. Try it and you'll create a toxic environment for both yourself and those you target or those who target you!

Imagine

Partnering with your power, clarity and well-being.

Affirmation

What I am going through now is part of my soul's process.
I am on a golden path.
The choices I make now are important.
I know the sun is shining on my intentions now
for personal growth and life lessons.

Chapter 8

Attachment to Results

(or view my message on YouTube)
https://www.youtube.com/watch?v=WcqXLiUU6Q0

When we're in alignment with what we're reaching for, we're on a journey of discovery.

So often, we're attached to the end results. Many times, we talk about things that evoke a response in others. In a previous chapter, we learned that no one is ever on the same wavelength as we are, even if we agree on some of the same issues. We still each have our own perspectives.

Most of us love in an exceptionally attached way. This can cause us to overstep our bounds, even unintentionally.

For example, our children may be called to move in directions we might fear, don't respect, or don't understand, yet we must let them fend for themselves. We can't shadow them every minute. They will make mistakes and we may not approve. We just need to remember that life experience is the best teacher.

Letting go happens gradually throughout life with our children until they're fully grown adults who no longer require our guidance. At this point, it's important to treat them as peers who may or may not seek our input into their lives. This allows them to fully appreciate the greatest gift parents can provide – their independence.

Society in general tends to give its attention to whatever is in the news or trending on social media. Inevitably, this evokes an emotional response. People look, see, respond or react, often on impulse. We need to use caution with what we see, read and hear around us. Then take responsibility for our own personal opinions and actions.

Most of us enjoy belonging to a group of like-minded people. We all want to be accepted for who we are, as we are. There's a kinship and we often don't feel so alone. We may feel admired, supported or encouraged. However, it's important to make our own decisions instead of listening to everyone else's opinions. If we just follow along without giving it any thought, we may wind up clashing with our own inner guidance. This is when we can make bad decisions.

Conversely, when we think thoughts that are passionate, happy, loving or eager, we are choosing thoughts in which the larger part of us is immersed. Instead of causing a separation between us and our Source, we create a partnership or relationship with power, clarity and well-being. We are in alignment with what we're reaching for.

Leave what everybody else thinks outside of the equation and line up with the story that the Source within whispers to you.

So how *do* you get on the other side of religious affiliations, social clubs, worldwide opinions, politics and other's considerations and follow through on being authentically yourself?

I hope your plans are to sift through variety, and come to personal clarity about what you prefer in life. Get your priorities figured out. Then come into alignment with your eternally evolving self for confirmation. Those around you will be watching!

Higher Consciousness moves through the minds of everyone, whether you're consciously aware of it or not. It's time to stop letting life happen *to* you and let life flow *through* you. This allows you to co-create a life of joyful and deliberate actions.

It is inherent. It is real. You know it resonates when you feel it. It is your truth. It is your inheritance as a person made in the image of your Eternal Identity.

From the longings of your heart, seek clarity and understanding that resonate within you through your emotions. Our feelings and emotions are the guidance system that help us know right from wrong. We must rely on the advice that comes from within as we get to know who we really are, on the inside.

It is in the silence that you will discover the lighted path. Cast your cares aside and allow great burdens to be lifted. Even if this reprieve is temporary, the confidence you will feel as you succeed in finding peace will assure a positive outcome towards any endeavor.

As one who walks with others on this planet, life will lead to the most profound experiences. You will attract fellow seekers who are also filled with joy. The path expresses itself through culture, custom, legacy, family, tradition, age, wisdom, life experience, revelation, celebration, children, jubilation, history and satisfaction, all of which are expressions of the life force within.

As humans, we are One, all on different journeys, but all moving toward our personal and planetary evolution. It's the beginning that has no end. The path unfolds eternally and is infinite in nature. Endless trails lead toward our eventual journey through eternity.

You want the best for yourself and others, don't you? You want to be healthy, play freely, feel supported, and nourished in mind, body and spirit. You want the best of friends and healthy relationships. You want to feel special and engaged in all sorts of wonderful activities that make life rich.

However, your goal should never be to control a situation or other person. That's impossible anyway. It's only natural to want to encourage and support your peers' quest to connect with their highest potential and the best way to do that is by your own example and how you live your life.

Competency ignites the broader knowledge they are reaching for that can only be found within themselves. No person will ever be able to offer counsel as powerful or as wise as the One within. So, let go of the outcome you have outlined for yourself and especially the outcome for someone else!

For example, there is no value in pointing a finger at your spouse or partner, expecting them to change so you will feel better. Change the way *you* feel about *them*.

My friend and motivational speaker, Lou Raja, posted a comment on LinkedIn recently that really hit home with me. He said, "Instead of saying, 'Here I am!', say 'There you are!'"

Support positive traits and let go of harmful behaviors, such as shame and blame. You can always expect the best without being attached to an outcome. When you begin to let go of the need to control someone else's behavior, you will relax and enjoy people as they are, and perhaps see that they are full of promise. Look for the positive traits in people!

Wisdom and understanding come from living your own life. It's not wise to compare yourself with others, even when you see people you might admire. They may serve as a source of inspiration for you. However, there really isn't such a thing as "overnight success." People in the news and limelight rarely reveal the years of heartache and struggle behind their "instant success."

Always remember that you hold the answers and solutions to your questions and problems inside you. That's where and how you create your own joyful and deliberate life.

Source energy understands your value and your part in the universal forward motion. The relationship between you and that which you have expanded within through effort increases with every realization of clarity. Come to know your physical attributes, through the fullness of your communing spirit. In this way, your contribution to humanity will manifest in surprising and delightful ways.

Your quest to learn, study and practice will propel you to be a consistent light. The ease with which your life flows will project a glowing radiance onto everyone you come in contact with. You've heard the saying, *"She lights up a room!"* This will be how others begin describing ***you***.

People looking on might not understand the process, but they will still be observing. If it feels good to them, they'll start asking questions you will be well-equipped to answer.

Without saying a word, people will be drawn to the pure, positive energy you can't help but emanate. You are aligned with the radiance within.

Source energy stands in love and appreciation for your availability, your presence. It requires effort, focus and determination to stay with an idea that is often not well-received by the masses. Transformation requires action only you can take.

Many people are slow to act out of fear of the unknown. They fear being judged, laughed at, scorned, even abandoned. People lean towards what is right in their own eyes. They often label others according to their own opinions and standards.

What other people say about you is none of your business. As you cultivate positive lifestyle habits, such as self-care, meditation and service to others, you begin to change the world around you by example. Your actions create a ripple effect, whether you realize it or not.

Step out of the box of conformity. Self-realization requires a paradigm shift. It means letting go of ideas and beliefs that you once held onto strongly, as well as ideas that still seem steadfast to others.

Imagine

Walking your own path
and not straying off onto other's paths.

Affirmation

I imagine how it feels to inspire and be inspired.

Pray. Prayer comes in many forms such as gratitude, appreciation, satisfaction, nature, resolution and non-resistance. As you resonate with your Eternal Identity, your path will light up on the way to greater joy. You know you're on track as you come to a sense of peace and contentment with your own thoughts.

Like me, you can feel it when you are being judgmental or unkind. Immediately change course to reflect an unwavering appreciation for others.

Understand your universal contribution to humanity. Realize and be grateful for your neighbor's gift to society as well. Your endeavors will show up on the faces of your peeps!

In the next chapter, we will explore the differences between confidence and conviction.

As you practice building on your qualities and abilities, self-assurance and trust will return. You will be certain of the truth. You will begin to eliminate stagnant patterns of thought and behavior. Ask any athlete. They have practiced running the race a million times in their heads before they have plunged into the pool or launched from a starting line.

Your willingness to put aside all distractions and quiet your mind allows you to hear the voice of your Inner Wisdom loud and clear. You can then explore all aspects of your life, with a keen focus on eliminating unproductive patterns.

Not only do you free yourself from limiting thoughts and behavior, your confidence and self-assurance will grow beyond measure. By tapping into your Inner Wisdom today, you can resolve any issues that could disrupt your calm and centered state of mind.

Imagine

Building on your qualities and abilities.
Self-assurance and trust will return.

Affirmation

*I reclaim my power and take back
emotional control of my life.
I make strong and self-directed choices.
I let go of doubt and allow my creativity to come forth.
I deserve to shine!*

Chapter 9

Conviction and Confidence

(or view my message on YouTube)
https://www.youtube.com/watch?v=egIDZYCUyeE&t=2s

Release self-doubt and put a stop to unwanted thoughts.

A lack of confidence comes from feelings of unworthiness. Unworthiness is activated by past experiences, as well as our connections with others. People are used to relating to each other moment by moment.

Most of us are on the lookout for a response from other people. How can we help it? Distractions are everywhere! A lot of us are people pleasers. At some point, we take orders and simply do what others want us to do. Many of us are afraid of what other people will think if we deviate from the way they've trained us. Others act out in rebellion. These examples are a few that determine and then fuel a lack of self-confidence.

Before going to sleep, it's especially helpful if you release any feelings of anxiety, fear, worry or doubt. With practice, you will get deeper and more restful sleep. Your chances of reviving an unpleasant thought when you first awaken will lessen considerably.

Be aware that the thoughts you give the most attention to before you go to sleep will begin again the moment you open your eyes in the morning. This is true, whether it's day or night. Whatever you focus on increases. That's why the things you fear have a tendency to actually happen – because you're always thinking about them! Train yourself to stop focusing on anything negative. Make a deliberate decision to focus on something wonderful and positive. That's when you can demonstrate the popular saying, "Change your thinking, change your life."

Before you put your head on the pillow at night, simply ask for a new path to reveal itself to you through the power of your subconscious mind. If you don't remember your dreams, be open to insights that occur anytime during the day. You simply have to be paying attention to the little "AHA" moments that arise.

Many times, you'll find that you wake up with a fresh idea. You'll be in a better mood. You'll have a chance to agree with the well-being that is *you*. Take specific actions. Squeeze that thought and get every drop of *deliciousness* out of it!

Let's get your day started right! When you wake up in the morning, say, *"Thank You!"* The best chance at boosting your confidence is during the first hour after you awaken.

Right after waking up, ignore your phone, don't answer your email, talk to no one. Make a commitment to yourself that you will spend the first moments of each morning going inside yourself to see or hear whatever wisdom comes.

Occasionally, I need to remind my husband that I take the first hour of the morning for myself (after hugs and cuddles, of course). That way, when he interrupts me, he won't be offended because we have agreed to this arrangement. My dear Jerry knows that it's extremely important for me to maintain this practice. Try this on your partner and see what kind of results you get.

You are worth it! The people around you will be much better served if you take care of your personal needs first! Relish in your decision. In the first golden hour of the day, take uninterrupted time for yourself, especially if you live alone. It is far too easy to launch into the next thing on your "to do" list when no one is watching. Be kind to yourself. Appreciate the dawn of the day. A new beginning.

Be mindful of things to be grateful for, like a hot shower, mint toothpaste on your toothbrush, a closet full of clothes to choose from, perfect health, feet to walk on and legs to take you where you want to go.

Confidence is built upon the satisfactory feelings of the wonderful things you have in place. If you can summon an attitude of feeling good, you're way ahead of the game. Each day is a clean slate. An opportunity to decide your future by setting an intention to feel prosperous, happy, blessed, fulfilled, lucky, and grateful, with an appreciation for what most people deem ordinary.

There's a saying that goes like this, "If I don't plan my schedule, someone else will plan it for me."

If you create a void in life, it must be filled. That's because the Universe hasn't previously had the space to fill your life with the good things you desire. Be careful to fill it with your own ideas, not somebody else's wishes for you. Set the intention to pay attention to which way your life is going.

I've found that the best way to prove my sense of worthiness is to understand my value as a person. Pay attention to holy promptings. Your guidance system will let you know that feeling good has countless benefits.

I start every day reading the following declaration, which has become my mantra. I invite you to take it as your own to read silently or say out loud in front of a mirror. Feel free to use this as a guide to create your own personal mantra. You can also substitute whatever word or words have personal meaning for you in the place of the Divine, God, Lord, Source, Higher Consciousness or other changes you may wish to make. Let this be a new starting point for you.

I am the best that I can be. I live in a way that is in harmony with my idea of the greatest good. I harmonize physically here in this body with that which I believe to be the best, or the good way of life!

*I am in the **flow** and consciously **attract** prosperity and abundance into my life. I am a cheerful and generous giver! I practice appreciation, gratitude and peace. I am **worthy** and **I align** with the Divine **Supply** who created me. I love and approve of myself. Everything always works out for me. I experience God's favor. I am **supplied** from an abundant and generous soulmate. I say **YES!** I feel **protected**. Angels and Guides, **I appreciate** that you walk with me and watch over me and remind me through intuition that **I AM** Well-Being. **I AM** truly blessed today. I model the life of Supply from the great **I AM**. How generous is our Creator!*

I Am wise.
I Am worthy.
I Am valued.
I Am blessed.
I Am protected.
*I Am in the **flow**.*
I Am highly favored!

*I allow the best of all things to **flow** effortlessly into my experience. Lord, thank you for unlimited increase in mind, money, body, talent and all other affairs!*

*I **imagine** my life the way I want it to be. All cooperative components are summoned. Even more important is that all components that are summoned will cooperate. It's the law.*

Abundant wealth blossoms all around me. I see value in my everyday life. I stand in well-being!
Thank you.

Confidence is inspired by thoughts gaining momentum in a forward motion. Practice being in sync with the ideas that are flowing. Stay as long as you can in a state of pure positive energy.

Before you know it, you will be inspired to take action on the best feeling thoughts, and your day will play out accordingly. Create a moving picture in your mind of the way you want your day and life to expand.

What do you want your day to look like? A conviction is nothing more than a firmly held belief or opinion. As humans, we often let other people define us, but it doesn't have to be that way.

If your commitment to yourself is pure and you're certain of what you want, you can create the future the way you desire it to be, but you must take control over your own thoughts, choices, and actions.

Get yourself into the habit of focusing on positive thoughts, then watch how the Universe supports you. As you acknowledge the small successes hour-by-hour, day-by-day, your confidence will grow. Before you know it, you'll be seeing larger successes happen in your life and you will know for certain that you can make your dreams come true.

You are on your way to becoming unstoppable! Nothing will get you down. Well, maybe a sneaky wave...we all get those. But you will have created a position for yourself where you'll be able to get back on your boogie board and ride the wave all the way to the shore!

The solution is to set clear intentions. Analyze what works for you and what doesn't get you the results you want. Adjust your thinking. Sometimes, this requires paddling against the current of the wave to get beyond the breakers. On occasion, you're going to get hit with a wave in the face. That's just part of the ride.

Undercurrents give us an opportunity, not only to survive, but thrive when we come out on the other side. Confidence is born from trial-and-error. If you're feeling insecure, it only means that you're focusing on the problem instead of the solution.

Your Eternal Identity never looks back. There is no history. There is nothing to rehash. Release regrets from your past. Forgive your indiscretions. The most powerful way to increase self-confidence is to keep your mind focused on forward motion.

Allow healing to take place. Appreciate yourself for the growth you are experiencing. Granted, you can't go back and undo wrongful deeds. Be aware that your small ego will often use self-talk to sabotage an attempt to achieve your ultimate goal. For me, this represents peace and contentment within myself. What would that look like for you?

You can improve newly found promises you've made to yourself with confidence when you invite thoughts about what is going right, not wrong. Get ready for some big changes!

Life supplies contrast and no one escapes. We live in a world based on dualities. You can't feel elation if you have never experienced despair. The cat dies. You fall and break your ankle. Your appointment doesn't show up. The deal you've been working on for months falls through. Life is filled with sorrows and losses, as well as happiness and joy.

There will always be two of you walking this path called Life: the Spirit that ushered you into the world, and the embodiment of that Spirit that we call the physical body. The Spirit knows the value and worthiness of your existence. Your body is simply a vehicle, a space of learning how to become the best version of yourself.

Abundance of Spirit is yours for the asking. Confidence is the relationship between the body you were born with, and trust and intimacy with the Divine. It is having the faith and belief that you can and will act in a right, proper and effective way. A certainty that you have the support you need to move toward success in every endeavor. Practice communion with the power and presence of your Eternal Identity.

Imagine

Being confident that your guidance system is in place.

Affirmation

I see evidence of my worthiness all around me.
I recognize the wealth of experiences that are
available to me as I draw near to the influence of the One.

In review, your day unfolds as you allow yourself to follow the promptings of your Inner Companion. You gain confidence as you walk the path of least resistance. Go with the flow. You can tell by the way you feel if you're on track or not.

Pat yourself on the back. Wrap your arms around yourself and give yourself a hug. Smile and laugh at yourself. You will see how good this feels and you'll want to incorporate this practice many times a day!

Your senses guide and direct you. Feel the wind on your face as you turn toward the sun. You are highly attuned to all the delights of this world that surround you. All you have to do is open your eyes. There are countless wonders right in front of you to appreciate and enjoy.

You start to attract only those things you desire to experience in your life. You allow no doubt to interfere with your conviction. You are sure in your beliefs. The steps you take toward clarity will work out for you.

You are often surprised by the contrasts you sometimes feel, but you know it's all part of an internal process. You may be used as a conduit for someone else's experience. What a privilege it is to be so!

Appreciate every opportunity to immerse yourself in a world of spontaneous variety. Life is exciting, wonderful and full of marvelous people, places, events and nature. You have so much to be grateful for: past experiences, present moments, future anticipations! Love being in your body!

While you sleep, all doubt is washed away. Each day is a white board on which you write your future, often in ways you cannot see right away. As you apply the principles outlined in this book, your foundation will become secure. And if your day doesn't exactly play out the way you intended, erase it!

We will take a look at deliberate thought in the next chapter. Let's define the word. According to the dictionary, to be deliberate results in a fully considered action done intentionally, not impulsively. Something decided in a careful and unhurried way.

Think of the last time you purchased a car. You laid out thousands of dollars toward a vehicle that you could trust and feel safe driving. You are certain to weigh all the options before spending all that money. You ask yourself many questions.

Does it have plenty of room in the back seat for the kids and car seats? What are the safety features? How many miles will this car get per gallon? Do I want to buy new or used? What are the warranty details? How much will insurance and regular maintenance cost?

You make the correlation between deliberate thoughts and feelings that occur. Only you know which way you want your personal momentum to flow.

Imagine

Being determined to follow through with consistent effort.

Affirmation

I pay attention to my structured plan, and I take daily action.
I am proud of my efforts, and I am richly rewarded
in the process of deliberate creation.

Chapter 10

Deliberate Thought

(or view my message on YouTube)
https://www.youtube.com/watch?v=6aHDurE32IA

E verything you see, taste, touch, smell and feel will have a lasting effect on your future. It's easy to get distracted in the age of Artificial Intelligence and other technology. Don't be persuaded to adopt someone else's idea of what is *perfect*.

Occasionally, I watch Verizon Prime on my iPad or on TV in the evenings. This channel offers a variety of movies on demand. What I enjoy about this network is that if a movie is not going in the direction I want to invite into my experience, I have the ability and opportunity to change channels immediately. I simply flip the switch between wanted and unwanted.

Try not to subject yourself to negative situations and circumstances.

In his book, *Good Vibes, Good Life*, Vex King states, "Good vibes are simply higher states of vibration. When you make an effort to raise your vibration, you show yourself the love and care you deserve."

Every good or bad experience you have in life comes to you by your careful consideration, no exceptions. We don't always make the right choices, but we always live with the cause and effect. We must bear the consequences of our actions.

Most people offer the majority of their thoughts in response to something they are observing. When you notice something wonderful, you feel wonderful. When you spot something awful, you feel awful.

It's important to remember that you alone are responsible for what you take in. The mind is amazing. It takes in all the information. It's not picky. It records it and that information is in the archives forever.

When I was fourteen, I went to see a movie called *The Exorcist* because all my friends were talking about it. What a mistake! I wish I knew then what I know now. I would never invite such horror today. The good news is, I learned a valuable lesson. Never subject yourself even remotely to a film that does not relay good feelings. The imprint of all thought remains on your mind indefinitely. All things that happen in your experience are a result of the request that you send out with your thoughts.

Do you believe you create your own reality by the thoughts you give your attention to? It's an interesting question, isn't it?

Most people walk around noticing what is going on around them. They believe their reality is the circumstances surrounding them. After all, you have eyes to see, ears to hear, and both often follow the loudest noise or distractions that grab your attention.

What you often think about is in response to an activity you are pursuing or are engaged in. Ask yourself, "Am I being action oriented? Or reaction oriented? Am I responding or reacting?" There's a difference. Reacting comes from being impulsive. Responding comes from taking the time to be intentional.

Consider this: A reaction is a person's ability to respond physically and mentally to external stimuli. Consider the element of surprise. When a person is surprised, all reason stops. If it's something positive you're reacting to, it's still an unconscious, uncontrolled thought that escapes your awareness.

When you react and notice by default what's going right or wrong in a situation, either way you are not in control of your mind or emotions.

By deliberate thought, you become sensitive to how you are feeling. See this as an opportunity to make partial or minor changes to improve the thoughts that are running through your mind. Is your observation of an event giving evidence of a wanted or unwanted outcome?

At this point, you have a chance to deliberately change the direction of your thoughts to something more in line with your true feelings. By applying grace to any given situation, you will immediately find relief.

Noticing how things are turning out for you is one clear way of understanding which energetic vibrations you're sending out. You always get the essence of what you are thinking about, whether you want to draw that thought to yourself or not.

Harvest from life the things that you prefer. The more you listen to the promptings of your Higher Self, the more you will realize your worthiness and choose from that place of understanding.

Changing a thought is simply letting go of the unpleasant one and replacing it with a more inspired emotion. It's an incremental rise. Focus is concentrating about where you want to put your attention. I've even gone so far as to write a list of my favorite things. I keep this list in my pocket so I can immediately find better feelings when necessary. You might consider doing something similar.

When you return to a more aligned space, take a moment to breathe deeply, then breathe again.

There is either harmony or discord between what you have going on vibrationally and what the higher version of yourself has going on. Your Inner Voice will never succumb to a lower energy that you might be hanging out in from your human perspective.

Acknowledge the benefits of releasing a negative thought. However, even though you can instantly change channels like you can with a remote control on your TV, the thoughts you leave behind can still linger, and must be allowed to incrementally disappear. This can only occur when you're paying attention to all your thoughts.

As you quiet your mind, you will return to a place of inner calm. You'll find yourself adding momentum to these better feelings. Soon enough, you'll realize that you really can control your thoughts and that it feels good!

Your Inner Being will continue to prompt you toward the path of least resistance. It will call you back to the control of your mind and emotions. Be patient and kind with yourself while you're practicing. Your Inner Being will always call you in the direction of what is highest and best for you.

Imagine

Closing the gap between the good feelings
you are having right now and what is unknown.

Affirmation

I attract beauty and joy
because this is what I focus on experiencing in my life.
I allow gratitude and appreciation to be my guides.

Focus on a more inspired thought.

Look for things to go right in your life. Decide to begin each day with this expectation. Chances are everything will work out for you as you align with love in all areas of your life.

From what we've covered in this book, you now understand that thoughts attract circumstances that manifest themselves into relationships, partnerships, chance meetings, and synchronicities! Struggle gives way to ease. You come to accept your worthiness as a human being. Now you realize that you are an heir to all that the Divine wants to provide!

Love precedes awareness. Love makes conscious choices. Love encourages control over the thoughts you think. The way you think determines the outcome of your day. Exercise your right to choose the direction of your thoughts in each moment.

Again, remember to be patient with yourself. Monitoring your thoughts takes practice. Know that this will get easier over time. Then all your good feelings will build momentum like a musical crescendo!

You will have a better chance to attract more opportunities to align with people, places, and experiences that are on the same wavelength as you are. These will be the "good vibes" you've heard about and probably felt. There is only forward motion. There is no need to carry the load of your past.

Shed all misgivings. Release all tension. Breathe deeply and expel any thoughts of regret or shame. The past is gone forever and can only be repeated by the thoughts you think in the present. Place yourself in a future role, wrapped up in cinnamon delight. In Divine Order, all is well!

Mmmmmmm…this feels wonderful and almost enchanting!

The next chapter leads us into a review of how to apply gracious living to yourself. Affirming statements are always part of the process. As you learn to adapt to new and fresh ways of looking at your life, transformation becomes a natural result. You will learn to strengthen trust in yourself by letting go of doubt and self-sabotage. Those feelings only serve to weaken you. Continue to take steps toward observing your thoughts and the things you constantly say to yourself. You will begin to love your life!

Imagine

Looking for circumstances and events
where you can apply gratitude and appreciation.

Affirmation

Whether I am young or old,
the opportunity for me to thrive is always possible.

Chapter 11

Let Go of Self-Doubt and Apply Gracious Living Toward Yourself

(or view my message on YouTube)
https://www.youtube.com/watch?v=L13gMgOdM34

No matter your age, it's never too soon to start appreciating yourself. You have skills and talents that belong to no one but you. You are an original!

Regular repetition of affirming statements encourages your brain to take positive affirmations as fact. This is called neuroplasticity because you're training your brain to create new pathways. You are literally rewiring your brain to think positive thoughts more frequently than negative or fearful, worry-based thoughts. Neuroscientists have proven this repeatedly so that it is now a well-established fact.

That's why your "self-talk" is so important. The brain doesn't know the difference between what is real and what is imagined. That's because the feelings behind those thoughts have energy, which is stored in your body's cells. That helps to explain why athletes rehearse events in their minds long before actually performing in their event. Artists and other creative people do the same thing. Even business people may rehearse a meeting in their minds before the actual event. That's because controlling your thoughts WORKS to bring about your desired results!

When you truly believe you can do something, your actions often follow.

Let go of doubt. Give yourself permission to dream a new dream. Then you will realize that you are limitless. If you don't believe in yourself, it's likely other people won't believe in you either. Every time you question yourself, every time you are afraid to fail, stop and take a moment to tap into your Inner Voice who will tell you the truth. You are worthy to receive anything you ask for, as long as it doesn't hurt you or anyone else.

As mortals, we will never be totally fearless, but we can determine to replace fearful thoughts by addressing them and then releasing them. Fear is often brought on by anxiety concerning the outcome of something you deeply care about. Maybe it's the welfare of a child, or uncertainty in the workplace. Perhaps you no longer have confidence in your marriage. Maybe you have been betrayed and are clinging to thoughts of unworthiness or being abandoned as a result.

Often, these thoughts are difficult to address without feeling a little down or depressed. Perhaps you are certain of the likelihood of something unwelcome happening. Attached is a feeling of dread. I get it. Been there, done that. At one time, I was even afraid of my own shadow!

Thick eye glasses were a permanent fixture on my face all through grade school. I was ridiculed and called four eyes more times than I can remember. Before I enrolled as a freshman in high school, I imagined how I wanted to present myself to fellow students. I let go of ridicule, got contact lenses, grew out my hair, bought some stylish clothes with babysitting money and launched into creating my new look. I took a chance and it was one of the best risks and investments I've ever made!

The thoughts you bring to mind and claim as your own are the first steps toward self-realization. Granted, it takes practice as we often are the first person to self-sabotage with thoughts like, "What will people think? Who do I think I am to be qualified for this position? I've never been a mother before! What if he doesn't like me?" All such thoughts are unfounded and are erroneous questions that should be guarded against. Those thoughts are not the truth of who you really are!

Many people want to attract a soulmate, friends, a dream college, a more appealing physical appearance, financial stability, peace of mind, and countless other experiences. There's an endless stream of well-being in all areas of life. It's all waiting for you to SAY TO YOURSELF AND TO THE UNIVERSE what you want your life to look like.

Push away your doubts and follow your intuition. Enter a new adventure of gracious living toward yourself and everyone else in your environment, including acquaintances, schoolmates, business associates and extended family.

As you talk about what you're passionate about, you'll begin to attract people who will hold a candle for your cause. They will take it into their hearts and carry a torch that will display a glowing light for all to enjoy. It will never be about the words you say, but how you make yourself and others feel, by the power of using affirmative thoughts.

Nothing is impossible in this world, and you can demonstrate it over and over to yourself. Wake up every morning with an undefeatable determination to prove that to yourself over and over again.

If you can stir up the fire in just one person's heart to follow their dream, the mission for your purpose in life will be fulfilled. Invite your Eternal Identity to help you set aside your cares and seek the powerful presence of true happiness.

Thank you for taking steps toward change. You are more than enough. You have so much to offer. You are inherently valuable. You are the best at what you do in your own way. You make a difference by being in this world.

Don't you just love being in control over your own mind? Isn't it fun to choose at every moment how you want to feel? Affirm goodness every chance you get. Look for circumstances and events where you can apply gratitude and appreciation.

Give thanks for every blessing. Be aware of the simple pleasures that give you joy. Life can be uncomplicated and complex at the same time. Life is always bringing contrast so you can affirm what it is you want to bring into your life.

Affirmations add value to all experience as you boost and support the Eternal Identity you want to partner with. You are a human being in the midst of a spiritual awakening. You are a person stepping into the reality of the Divine. Appreciate the gifts you have been given. As you give these gifts away, they come back to you full circle.

Love your life and all the people you encounter. Appreciate the simple pleasures you enjoy through your senses. They carry a great price and yet they are free! Sounds that thrill you. Scents that tantalize you. Visions of loveliness. The touch of a child's small hand in yours. The sweet taste of honey on your lips.

You have everything you need to enjoy this life, gifts that are from the Universe, delivered to you, especially for you, in all splendor and magnificence. Even in death, you see beauty, knowing that the spirit within will live on, and on, and on.

In the next chapter, we will look at satisfaction as a way to expect fulfillment of what you have been yearning for. Your dreams can come true. It's up to you to fully develop your own individual strength and reality that will support your desires.

Although each person has their own expectations of the way they want their world to spin, often it doesn't include you and your expectations! All of us have beliefs that get in our way. Ask yourself, "How am I responding to this situation? Is this true for me or am I simply observing behavior?" You can tell the difference by whether you feel satisfied or not.

Quit arguing for your limitations, the inner critic that says, "Who do you think you are?! You're not qualified to do *that!*" Your Supplier, who inspired you to do the work, will never let go of your dreams. Don't delay updating and replacing any false belief that's stopping you.

It's easy for your angels and guides to know what's possible for you. Until *you* decide *you* want to feel more satisfaction, until *you* find passion and resonance with what *you* know to be *your* desires, until *you* let go of those looking at you from the peanut gallery… only then will you truly understand the process of what it means to change your thinking and change your life. It's between you and you.

Imagine

Your expectations will not always be met
coming from an outside source.

Affirmation

*Let me model peace, appreciation,
harmony and happiness.
Let me wear a constant smile.
I look at the blessings in my life
with joy, satisfaction and gratitude.*

Chapter 12

Can We Ever Be Satisfied?

(or view my message on YouTube)
https://www.youtube.com/watch?v=s6odtqyyLkc

Y ou are the only one who creates your experience. No one else. Everything that comes to you comes by the power of your thoughts. Now, don't get mad. You might say, "Sure, it's easy for him to say, he's got the boat, the car, the soul mate, the dream job…"

Let's take this one step at a time.

Satisfaction can be defined as a fulfillment of one's wishes, and it often revolves around the people we meet and greet. To be expected, families we are born into and the social aspects of living in a world with other people often collide.

It feels good to be accepted and valued by the people we care about. However, remember that there truly is great pleasure derived from the gratification that you and only you are responsible for.

What you feel is owed to you or due you will only hinder any contentment that satisfaction brings, especially in the reparations of an injustice or wrong-doing. While validation from important people in your life is wonderful, it can never replace the pride you feel when your own self-worth is strong. You want to create a stable foundation to boost your confidence, trust and belief in yourself.

By first turning your attention within, you affirm that you are worthy and valuable regardless of anything you do. As a result, you develop an unshakable belief in yourself and your abilities. Only then will the validation you receive from others be a pleasant complement to your own strong sense of self-realization.

Circumstances and events will occur that give you evidence of how you're doing. Relax, all is well. Agree with the conclusions you have drawn. Believe it first and *then* see it!

Be content with what you have control over right now.

By being delighted in your value as a human being, you develop a steadfast sense of self-worth and confidence, regardless of the praise or criticism you receive from others. People tend to base their perceptions of worthiness on the feedback received from someone other than themselves.

This tendency is often nurtured in children by parents or guardians in their attempts to satisfy a resolution to raise children properly. You then learn to believe yourself only to be valuable when others say they approve of you.

As you honor yourself for who you are as a person, rather than by the actions you take, your satisfaction will be fed by the development of a strong sense of accountability. It will provide you with a powerful sense of self-acceptance that fills you with confidence and joy.

Your balanced approach to the fulfillment of your objectives will help you recognize all the factors that contribute to your ability to pursue your course in life successfully. Stay true to yourself.

Satisfaction comes from having a desire and then moving in the direction of it.

I started writing this book two years ago. I was inspired by the Divine Light to take dictation from benevolent sources. I call these forces Soloman and Magi, two guides who introduced themselves to me on New Year's Day.

Both figures represent scribes. Meditation was the key to the doorway that unlocked my subconscious mind. I surrendered to it and wrote every day for several hours until I was instructed to stop. I concluded the messages I received on May 31st of the first year, but that was just the beginning. Birthing a book is a lot like birthing a baby. It needs time to incubate.

The journey toward something desired is always more satisfying than actually getting there. As you move your thoughts toward your goals, your actions gain momentum. When you're gaining speed toward something you're already excited about, that in itself produces satisfaction, clarity, assurance and well-being.

Even though you might not know exactly what steps to take to reach your goals, those steps will come in time as you stop doubt and resistance before they can take hold and attach themselves to your thoughts.

It's enough to be content along the journey because that might be all you can do right now. Ideas for your next steps along the path will light up to lead the way.

You always have the power to turn your thoughts around to a more positive focus. You're at an advantage if you can catch the supervision of your thoughts. Turn in the direction of the way you want your next steps to flow.

As you take control over the activation of your thoughts, you soon become invincible. Your Inner Being will offer what you are ready to hear.

The power is in finding the feeling of a more elevated idea. Satisfied and more, satisfied and more, satisfied and more. When an impression is activated within you, and you have no contradictory thoughts to it, the momentum will carry you to the end result.

Imagine

Being enough just as you are!

Affirmation

*I allow myself to stay in the place
of satisfaction with ease and grace.
I purposely bring my mind to a state
of allowing all good to flow to me,
which I gratefully accept.*

Appreciate all the things that are going right for you. Accept and value yourself just the way you are. You are enough.

You are not what you do, nor are you the things that happen to you. Rejoice in your personality. Celebrate all the gifts you have to share with the world. You are worthy of your own abilities. Honor yourself for those attributes that belong only to you. Make a list! What are you good at? Where do you shine? What do you enjoy?

Be assured that you are moving in the direction of your desires, but they need to be clarified first. Agree with the Eternal Identity inside you that you are already balanced and fulfilled. You don't have to reach outside yourself for validation because you know the satisfaction you feel right now gives you the assurance that you are on the right track.

Release any doubts you have surrounding the ideas that have formed in your mind. Get excited about the confidence this inspires! The full manifestation is on its way. Be eager to see how the next step presents itself. You are in the perfect frame of mind to allow your dreams to come true.

By being satisfied in the moment, you gain access to the adventure about to unfold. Tell the story of the way you want your day to unwind. Keep these thoughts within reach. If you embrace the concepts outlined in this book, you can be confident that the Inner Hero you co-create with is your biggest cheerleader.

You have a great advantage as you catch the direction your thoughts are taking you. Imagine being an origami sailboat, light as a feather, being carried downstream. There might be turbulence, but you will be guided around the rocks and disturbances in the water. All power is in maintaining a satisfied outlook. There is no tension in satisfaction. Your desires will gain momentum and grow without hindrance.

In the next chapter, I will take you through a guided meditation. You will find an aid to strengthen your sense of protection and comfort in this practice.

One good way you can apply the feeling of inner security is by allowing it to help you dissolve old fears and blockages that may have seemed too intimidating in the past.

During a period of meditation, simply focus on expanding your mind and distancing your perspective on your life. See if any limiting patterns jump out at you or if any other tendencies seem to pull your attention. By affirming that your Inner Wisdom protects and guides you through every experience, you will be able to work through old issues and resolve them.

Imagine

Looking within.

Affirmation

*I make relaxation and meditation part of my daily life.
Peace and quiet bring me clarity and joy.*

Chapter 13

Meditation

SCAN ME

(or view my message on YouTube)
https://www.youtube.com/watch?v=AYLBWv2wp1g

Many of you who are reading this book are either familiar with or have already heard about the value of meditation. Do you practice it? Meditation is the exercise of focused concentration that brings the body back to the present moment over and over again as we release limiting thoughts when they come into mind.

The use of meditation has been scientifically proven to be a valuable tool helping to reduce anxiety, chronic pain, depression, heart disease and high blood pressure. Meditation promotes emotional health and enhances self-awareness. It can actually lengthen your attention span as you let go of the scattered thoughts of the "monkey mind."

Use meditation as a tool to quiet your mind. As you seek freedom from distractions, you can hear the still voice within. As you lose yourself in reflection, it becomes your default pattern of thinking.

Enjoy the freedom in this as you choose to review circumstances you currently face. During meditation, you can gently let them go. Discover the answers to questions cycling through your mind. They are being revealed to you as you surrender your will to the Divine Mind. Can you be present to the fullness of your true value and worth? How can you bring completeness to your life?

Answers won't necessarily pour into your mind while you're in a relaxed state of meditation. I received information from two of my spirit guides while sitting in our hot tub! The information you seek will likely come when you least expect it, but pay attention! You might not recognize the answer immediately.

As you surround yourself with serenity and silence, without distractions, you perceive the wisdom of your Eternal Identity. The Inner Voice knows more about what is right for you than any external source or person. The answers to your personal quandaries are found within rather than outside yourself. We know this to be true. There is no need for you to seek other opinions.

The wisdom gained through reflection and meditation will inspire the best path and course of action to take. Trust these insights. Acknowledge that understanding yourself in the highest inner realm is a powerful tool.

Dive deep into your soul and disregard the self-deprecating voices that attempt to block your progress. Your Eternal Identity will reveal those answers to you at exactly the right time in the depths of your heart and mind...as soon as today!

Meditation allows you to enjoy a heightened sense of intuition.

Knowing the signs of intuition is just like any ability and, with practice, you can improve your skills and make the most of them to reach a level of mastery in your life.

Through meditation, you enjoy a heightened sense of instinct. It helps you navigate through tricky situations more easily. Find a quiet place to be alone and let your thoughts about the day-to-day nuances just flow downstream.

If something is really important for you to remember, imagine putting those thoughts in a paper bag and place the sack on the floor near your feet where you will be able to retrieve it once the meditation is complete.

This gives you assurance that you won't lose anything important. In this way, you enhance the ability to get better connected to your spiritual center so you can activate direct communication with your Inner Guide.

Imagine reaching deep within yourself to tap into the intelligent energy at your core. This energy is a tangible force that heightens your awareness and connects you to the stream of timeless wisdom that the Universe makes available to you.

All of us need guidance during the course of our day. As you quiet your mind, you awaken your sense of inner awareness. By following the strands of subtle prompts, your Spiritual Self will guide you in all your decisions. Meditation strengthens the awareness of your connection to Universal Wisdom. It can open your mind and enhance your intuitive sensitivity.

Your level of knowledge is not limited to the finite nature of the physical body. You are a spiritual being and you are interconnected with Divine Wisdom. You have the ability to tap into your Eternal Identity and use the insights you gain to take actions in creating a more fulfilling life.

Meditation requires consistent practice. Begin with fifteen minutes daily, or even less. It takes about a month to establish a new habit. So, even if you *go through the motions daily*, you teach your mind to return to the activity. If you miss a day, it will feel like you're missing out on something very valuable. Be patient as you start training yourself to quiet your mind. There will be great benefits to you in this disciplined effort alone.

As you develop a stronger connection to Divine Wisdom, you will further strengthen your intuition and develop a higher purpose of spiritual clarity. Without resistance, in the lucidness of a sound mind, you will find yourself in the midst of your Eternal Identity.

Imagine

Being in the midst of a calming exercise.

Affirmation

*Today is my day to express the Universe's
potential through me.
I will share it in my own unique way with the world.*

Our thoughts are the gateway that allows the energy that we *are* to flow toward our desires. As you quiet mental pictures of scattered activity, you make space for those positive, rewarding ideas to flow and be received.

At this time, I would like to lead you through a guided meditation. Instead of elevating your thoughts, relax into a feeling of detachment.

A Calming Exercise

Although you have many teachers to draw from, you will always come from your own perspective. You are assured. Inspiration is whispering to you. You feel comfortable.

Release any thoughts now that may inhibit you from feeling relaxed. Relax your forehead. Feel the muscles in your face releasing the tension you didn't even know you were holding. Get into a comfortable sitting position. Close your eyes. Breathe deeply several times, inhaling for five seconds through your nose with your mouth closed, then exhaling for five seconds with or without an "*AHHHH*" sound with an open mouth. Soon, you will feel settled and comfy.

Meditation

Breathe deeply and exhale slowly for thirty seconds. You feel more calm with each breath you take in, and let out. Relax your shoulders. Feel all the tension in your arms draining away. As you quiet your mind, all resistance drops away.

Gently release stray thoughts and focus on your breathing.

You are beginning to feel weightless as you release the tension in the muscles in your back. Move this feeling of release down through your seat and thighs. You are feeling more and more relaxed.

There is nothing more important for you right now than to appreciate the stillness of your body in this tranquil state. You deserve these few precious minutes all to yourself. Your body is responding to the joy of simply being. You are sensitive to the way this high frequency feels in your body.

You feel peaceful. You are relaxed. Allow all the things you have asked for to trickle gently into your experience. At this very moment, allow yourself to completely relax and receive. Allow yourself to come to a place of heightened sensitivity. It feels like you are detached from your body. Your body seems to vanish because you are so much more than your physical body. This serenity feels so good!

Here you are, in a state of allowing Source energy to flow through you. You are being cleansed. You feel energized. Without effort and in complete surrender, be blessed.

You are worthy. You are relaxed. Breathe in. Breathe out. All tensions melt away. Appreciate this state of stillness. You see the tremendous value of this experience. Breathe in, release. Breathe out, release. You shall not lack for whatever you need to become the person you choose to be.

Breathe in, release. Breathe out, release. Breathe in, release. Breathe out, release. Relax. Let go. Just *BE*.

Thank You, Thank You, Thank You.

Epilogue

SCAN ME

(or view my message on YouTube)
https://www.youtube.com/watch?v=1CX2eAFVTX8

I t has been a pleasure sharing this information with you. It is my hope that you will come to the knowledge of your own truth without outside interference as we have discussed in the previous chapters.

The life you dream about is closer than you may think. I encourage you to reach for each detail with an open heart and increasing courage. Step into each Principle of change, transformation, and adaptability with your new self-realization. In doing so, your dreams will be ignited with warmth, appreciation, satisfaction and love. Remember, you are the one you have been waiting for. Celebrate your success!

Imagine

What it feels like to practice the principles
of a spirit-supplied life.

Affirmation

My intentions are clear and unconflicted.
Whatever I am working on,
I know that I am capable of achieving.
I know that I deserve it.
I am worth my own time and effort.
The new beginning I seek will come
with my own focus and patient determination.

What makes a
Master of Alignment?

How does one become a master?

You become a Master of Alignment when you match up with your Eternal Identity. You become a master by using your imagination to practice tuning yourself to that which is within you, your Higher Consciousness.

As you adjust your vantage point until love is what you feel, no matter the circumstances, you have mastered alignment. You must find a way to focus yourself in the world as it is, not ask the world to change so that you can focus or feel better. You have to care about releasing negative thoughts, even though it might be a difficult thing to do. Make a promise to yourself that you will commit to becoming a master of your own thoughts and the creation of your life.

Mastery is living in the world and maintaining an even energy. You can't keep running into a cave of isolation and hiding. This will only lead to despair. You've got to come out and live in the world because the world needs you to shine your light in the only way *you* can!

You achieve this by fostering a consistent state of gratitude and appreciation. You can also apply meditation and let your good feelings rise. Then focus on your thoughts. Catch doubt before it can take hold of you. Then meditate again and see how much further you're able to get.

Be grateful for all the positive experiences that are in your life each and every day. Allow your feelings to let you know when you're in a state of alignment and then milk it for everything you can!

When you decide you want to feel good (in alignment with your Eternal Identity), goodness is all you will be able to attract. When attacked, turn the other cheek! Let adversity bounce off you. Be willing to change and adapt to more emotional security. With self-realization comes an understanding of the deeper meaning of life. *Your* life.

Align, live, notice, adjust, look for the feelings that feel good (God) just for the feelings of being in harmony with your Eternal Identity. Your Inner Hero will take you the rest of the way. Reach for the tactile sense of it until you're sure of your ability to center your attention on what you know to be true for *you*. This is called mastery.

Masters are confident in their abilities to focus with ease and flow. Mastery in meditation results from self-discipline and practice, and ultimately feels as natural as breathing. There is no effort.

It's important to realize that most people in a waking state are not in alignment with who they truly are. That's a very important piece of information! Guard your heart against outside influences. Look at a person's face. It will give you all the information you need to know about them in any situation. Expressions are telling!

True masters trust their connection with their Inner Being, their Eternal Identity, so that at any point in time they can be anywhere and not be affected by the low vibrations of others around them.

They watch their self-talk. They practice imagining favorable scenarios throughout the day. They put sticky notes of positive affirmations in places where they will be reminded, such as the bathroom mirror or the dashboard of the car.

Mold your expectations to agree with the story you want to tell. Then take yourself out into the world. Be the love and others will reflect that back to you. In this way, you will be a blessing and you will attract blessings and be of value wherever you are.

I ask that the Source within me become the dominant relationship in my life, which enables me to have power over my own thoughts and actions so that I can then be of the highest value and service to others.

This is the highest elevated mantra from me as my gift to you, but you can choose to write your own. Never take your eyes off the relationship with your Eternal Identity.

Your Eternal Identity is paving the way before you, believing in you, encouraging you, knowing that you can be, do or have anything your heart desires. Look for reasons to be optimistic. Be satisfied. Imagine. Make lists of positive aspects. Hold your attention on what's going right!

If you want to be an influencer; if you want to be a light for someone who is in the darkness, you must practice and model happiness. There is no running away from the inevitable. We all live in this world, but we can each choose where we focus our thoughts and attention. Let's choose to create a world that works for everyone, where we can all enjoy peace, harmony and fulfillment, a world where we are all accepted for who we are, as we are.

Hold your own vibration at the highest level. This is what true upliftment is. It's catching a glimpse of the divinity in a person and what they really want, which is peace and freedom. As you hold that image for another clearly, they will then catch a glimpse of it and begin to heal.

You will always be a benefit to others as they feel your unconditional love for them. Bring out the best in people. Be an example of what they want to experience for themselves. This is what teaching is, and we are all teachers for each other.

This is what bliss feels like. This is living happily ever after. This is living a life of Supply. This is being a Master of Alignment. You have a choice at every moment in deciding what reality you want to create.

Alignment is the way to successfully living with your Eternal Identity. You will find it easier with practice. Alignment will turn you toward confidence. Alignment will turn to empowerment, invincibility, certainty, and connection with the true Source of your being. As you master your thoughts, you master your life! Move in the direction of your Eternal Identity. It is the gateway to a precious and fulfilling life.

Acknowledgments

Writing is a solo sport but, with that said, it takes a team to create a book. For years, I have enjoyed unyielding support from my husband, Jerry Dalke, who has bolstered my creative side on so many levels. Jerry, you are the flip side to my coin. It doesn't seem to matter where I am in a state of passion, you have taught me well the power of FOCUS, for which you are famous!

In appreciation for my Sissins, Melanie Payton and Kelly Harland, both of whom I get my spiritual therapy from in a monthly phone call.

To my mentors, the Channeling Chicks from my Hay House writers group: Julie Jin, Lesley Corte, Margot Schaal, Jennifer Juniper and Denise Holland. Super intelligent women aligned with the practices and implementations outlined in this book.

Many thanks to Rev. Denise Landes who is a magnificent book coach. I am grateful for her careful eye for detail and her spiritual reverence for the message conveyed. I appreciate the countless hours we invested over the table reading aloud. A MUST for any writer!

I want to express my appreciation for the gifted and experienced teacher and media specialist I have had the privilege to work with over the years, Joanne McCall, *The Media Polisher*. Her insights, wisdom, boot camp training and recent book release, *Media Darling*, were responsible for the path I am now on.

To put it all together, I could not have done it without Norma-Jean ("NJ") Strickland, Chief Visionary Officer and Executive Producer of Starlight Creative Productions, LLC, and an established author herself. NJ worked tirelessly to organize, edit, address format issues, spelling, punctuation, research, grammar, tenses and flow. NJ is a one woman design team!

I appreciate the many transformational non-fiction writers who have paved the way for me to learn and grow in my faith. Contemporary teachers as well as those who have closed the door on life and have launched on a new adventure. Men and women from whose array of written resources I have drawn on time and time again.

Thank You, Thank You, Thank You!

I have been a student for life. I first made the agreement to align with the Divine back in 1991.

I became a seeker when I was introduced to nature. It was in the wilderness where my husband and I first heard the angels sing. My husband has been my lifelong companion through many physical and mental challenges.

As a result of watching him during his own struggles, I have learned to live by the Supply of the All Divine. The Divine takes many forms. I connect to the ultimate Source of help, and realize my full value as a human soul who is constantly evolving.

I have found that my own sense of truth is ultimately the most important element in processing the information I take in from outside sources. It's part of the wonder of being alive. It's a privilege and an honor. I am extremely grateful for my life experiences, and to my teachers, I say, "Amen!"

About the Author

Voyager of Bliss and Creativity, Julanne Dalke is a writer committed to helping others find freedom to follow their faith-based path. She is also a professional voice actor, painter, and meditative studies class facilitator. Her company, *What's Your Story,* produces audio publications that honor and celebrate individuals by listening to and preserving their stories.

Julanne holds certificates of education in the fields of meditation, writing, and public speaking. Julanne holds a certificate of completion for over 5,000 hours of volunteer service as a radio personality for outstanding contributions to Recreational Reading for the Blind from Katie Hobbs, Governor of Arizona.

Julanne is the facilitator and founder of *Free to Be* for in-home meditative studies.

Julanne has written and delivered numerous speeches and holds many awards for exceptional achievement in the Toastmasters International Communication program.

A strong relator, Julanne specializes in the area of encouragement. She allows the spirit of increase to express itself through prolific writing. Julanne believes that, as you learn to trust the wisdom of your heart and make creative choices based on what you know to be true and right for you, the process becomes progress.

Contact Information

julannedalke@yahoo.com
julannesmusings.blogspot.com (Whispers of the Heart)
http://www.vfademos.com/JDalke
https://www.linkedin.com/in/julanne-dalke-484a904
https://www.youtube.com/@julannedalke8719
https://www.instagram.com/julanne.dalke/
https://www.facebook.com/profile.php?id=100078882204111

NOTES

NOTES

NOTES

www.ingramcontent.com/pod-product-compliance
Lightning Source LLC
Chambersburg PA
CBHW071402120626

46546CB00002B/787

To my love, Camille

Thank you for helping me find my wings.
I couldn't have done this without your love and support.
You are, and always will be, my greatest leap.

CONTENTS

Heart Connection Meditation

Start With Stillness

Before diving into the book, take a moment to pause. Let go of the noise, return to the present, and reconnect with your heart.

This free 5-minute guided meditation was created to help you connect with your inner voice and begin this journey from a grounded, centered place. Come back to it anytime you need clarity, calm, or a moment of peace.

Visit the link or scan the QR code below to access the meditation:

heart.daniellebongiorno.com

There's an additional resource in the back of the book when you're ready to dive even deeper.

INTRODUCTION

RISK-TAKER

Those who don't jump will never fly.
—Leena Ahmad Almashat

I made it halfway up the cliff before my nerves kicked in. I looked around and saw children a third of my age climbing to the top and fearlessly jumping into the clear, turquoise water, but something inside of me held me back.

We had spent the day at Waimea Bay, watching kids and adults leap from the cliff on the far side of the beach. Finally, my partner said, "Will you jump with me?" My immediate reaction was, "Absolutely not." I've never been much of a risk-taker and typically prefer my feet planted firmly on the ground. However, when I saw how many children were jumping, I thought, *If they can do this, so can I.* So, I hesitantly agreed.

My partner and I began the walk to the cliff. You could see her excitement building as we drew closer, while uncertainty started to rise in my gut. I realized how much taller it looked up close than it had from my towel 100 yards away. Despite my nerves kicking in, I found the courage and started the climb. With each step, the fearful voice inside of me grew louder and louder until, finally, it convinced me to turn around. I climbed back down, weaving through the kids as they made their way up, and placed my feet safely back in the sand.

Meanwhile, my partner was nearing the top and was preparing to make her leap. She looked down at me one more time with a big smile on her face. She wrapped one arm around her body, plugged her nose, and jumped! As she came out of the water, there was pure joy and accomplishment on her face. She did it. She took the leap.

I didn't take the jump that day because I was afraid—afraid to fall. I listened to fear instead of courage, and for too long, I had done the same in my life. Fear had called the shots, keeping me bound to a life that didn't fulfill me instead of stepping into the life tugging at my soul. But I finally reached a point in my life where enough was enough. I was done letting fear dictate my choices. I was tired of standing on the edge, afraid to fall, instead of believing I could fly. If I wanted to live the abundant, authentic life I dreamed of, I had to be bold enough to **take the leap**.

How did I arrive at this point? What spurred this newfound boldness? It was two realizations. The first was that if I continued walking the path I was on, I wouldn't be living a life that was truly and authentically me. The second was that everything I wanted was on the other side of my fear. Fear is what kept my feet anchored to the ground for too long and led me to believe that if I leaped, I wouldn't fly. I reached a point in my life where I had to ask myself if I was going to let fear continue to call the shots or pursue the life that was nudging me. I didn't know what would happen after I leaped, but I knew if I stayed where I was, I might regret it for the rest of my life.

Less than 5 years ago, my life looked nothing like it does today. To start with, I was married to a man. I held a successful, six-figure-paying job. I was living a life that looked great on paper, while deep down, I was searching for more. In addition to all that, I was afraid to trust myself, unsure of what I truly wanted, and struggling to fully accept who I was. I longed for greater freedom and the joy that comes from living a life that felt right for me. I knew there was a better path waiting, but I didn't expect that path to lead me in the direction that it did. It was during this time of searching that I faced one of the most significant decisions of my life: whether to stay in my marriage or end it and start a completely new life.

No one enters into a marriage thinking divorce will be the end result. You carry hopes and dreams for a future you're going to build together. Accepting that this may not happen is one of the most challenging realities to come to terms with. What was even harder was knowing that I would be the one choosing to go in another direction. After 5 years of marriage, I came to a fork in the road. I was married to a man while falling in love with a woman. This didn't happen overnight. What started as a friendship blossomed into attraction, and over time, it turned into love. I reached a point where I knew I couldn't deny this any longer, and I would have to make decisions about what this meant for my life.

This wasn't the first time I'd felt attraction to another woman or questioned what I wanted, and to be completely honest, it wasn't the first time it came up while I was married. A few years earlier, I developed feelings for a female friend but handled the situation poorly. I hid and lied because I was so afraid to admit my feelings and even more fearful of what this might mean for my life. That experience taught me hard lessons, and I vowed never to repeat it. So when this attraction came up again, I chose honesty. I told my husband about my feelings, and while it wasn't easy to hear, he met me with understanding. He gave me space to process and explore what this meant for me and our future.

I carried heavy, looming questions about my sexuality and even heavier questions about what this would mean for my marriage, but beneath it all was a consistent longing. I longed to accept myself fully and to confidently be able to say, "This is who I am, and this is the life I want to live." I longed to let go of the opinions and expectations that I had allowed to influence me for too long. I wanted to make decisions based on what I wanted, not what I thought I "needed" to do or "should" do. And most of all, to release the fear holding me back and discover what it would feel like to fly. It didn't take me long to realize that this was so much more than deciding my sexuality or whether I wanted to be with a man or a woman; it was about learning to fully accept who I was and embrace the life I was meant to live.

AUTHENTICITY

*Authenticity is the daily practice of letting go of
who we think we're supposed to be and embracing who we are.*
—*Brené Brown*

In the book *The Top Five Regrets of the Dying*, Bronnie Ware shares her experiences with individuals in their final days. She asked if they had any regrets or would live their life differently, and the most commonly spoken regret was this: "I wish I'd had the courage to live a life true to myself, not the life others expected of me".[1]

I read those words over and over again. They echoed a truth I was beginning to uncover in my own life. I wanted more than anything to live a life true to myself, and I knew if I didn't, I would look back and carry this same regret.

For me, living authentically means living in alignment with who we are and the unique path that has been created for us. When our lives don't align with our beliefs, values, or personal desires, it is a clear sign that we aren't living true to ourselves. Sometimes, we end up here because we've allowed outside voices to drown out our inner guidance. At other times, the fear of letting others down feels stronger than the joy of living a life that honors who we are, or maybe we've never taken the time to ask ourselves what we really want and discover our truth.

When we're living out of alignment, tension builds. It can manifest as a struggle to find peace, a yearning for a deeper purpose, or simply the feeling that there's more to life than what we're currently experiencing. If this tension becomes strong enough, it will propel you to examine your life on a deeper level and consider what needs to change. For me, this played out in my marriage and then a few years later in my career. For you, this may look like staying in a job that drains you, holding back on a big life change for fear of letting others down, or ignoring the quiet ache inside that tells you you're not living in alignment with your true self.

Perhaps you've been people-pleasing, living up to expectations, or following a path that doesn't ignite passion within you. The tension you feel is a powerful signal that change is needed, and there's more for you than the life you're currently living. It's an invitation to reflect and ask yourself, *Is this the life I truly want, or is it time to make a change?*

As I began to embrace my authentic self, I realized that certain aspects of my life no longer aligned with the person I was becoming, so I took bold steps toward creating a life that reflected who I wanted to be. It wasn't easy, but I could no longer continue down the path I was on while knowing there was more for me.

Authenticity begins within. It starts with the bold decision to accept yourself fully, speak your truth without hesitation, and pursue your dreams with unwavering courage, regardless of the doubts, opinions, or obstacles in your way. This is the journey that changed my life, and it can change yours too.

When you think about the life you're living today, does it feel like the life you want? Is there an ache in your heart for something more? A dream you've been afraid to pursue? A longing to live in a way that feels more aligned with your soul? What if I told you that all of this is possible? You just need to be willing to listen to your heart, release your fear, see through the eyes of faith, and, just maybe, take that courageous leap.

If you're ready to live the life you've always dreamed of, I invite you to take this journey with me. I promise, there's so much waiting for you on the other side.

PREPARING TO LEAP

Every great move forward in your life begins with a leap of faith…
—Brian Tracy

When I started my journey, I had no clue what would be waiting for me after I took my leap. I had hoped for something beautiful, but there were days when I questioned everything I was doing. Looking back on that time, I see clear steps and defining moments that shaped my process.

I've taken multiple leaps over the years—in my relationships, my career, and in bringing my truest self to the world. I've learned what it takes to move forward when fear is loud and the future feels uncertain. I've lived through it, so I understand the challenges you will face and want to help prepare you for what to expect along the way.

What emerged through my transformation is what I now call the **LEAP Method**: a four-part courage-building process that helped me move from fear to freedom and live out the truth my heart was calling me to.

Listen to your heart.

Reconnect with your inner knowing and quiet the noise around you.

Embrace your faith.

Build the trust to move forward, even when fear and doubt feel loud.

Accept your truth.

Release shame and own what's real and right for you.

Pursue your path.

Take bold, courageous steps toward the life that's calling you.

Each part of this book explores one of these themes in depth, offering personal stories, reflections, and heart-led wisdom to support you through your own leap.

I've learned that taking the leap isn't just a one-time act; it's a journey that transforms you, challenges you, and calls you higher. This book is here to guide you through that process every step of the way. By the end, I hope you'll feel more grounded in who you are, clear on what you want, and empowered to create a life that feels honest, true, and free.

THEN YOU FLY

I've never jumped out of a plane, but the leaps I've taken in my life have felt just as heart-pounding, terrifying, and freeing. To understand what skydiving is actually like, I spoke with people who had taken that plunge, and their stories amazed me. So much of what they described mirrored the emotional journey of "taking the leap" in my own life.

Most of them described the build-up the same way: You arrive, meet your instructor, watch a short video, sign waivers, and get briefed on what to expect. Then you get on the plane, and it begins taking you up. Most said this is where the nerves kicked in, and things started to feel real. "I was terrified the whole way up," one person told me.

When you finally get to the jumping altitude, you make your way to the opening of the plane. Your feet dangle over the edge, and your tandem partner (a trained professional strapped to your back) is all that's keeping you from falling. There's no turning back. Just one simple instruction: "Breathe. Lean forward. Fly."

What follows is a moment of pure surrender. The free fall is exhilarating and even terrifying at first, but then unexpectedly blissful. One woman said, "Nothing prepares you for the rush you feel when you're falling." It's an incredible moment of pure surrender and bliss. There's nothing you can do but surrender to the moment and simply be. You can see the curve of the earth stretching for miles, and for a brief time, you are limitless, and life is *limitless*.

Finally, the parachute deploys, and you realize you aren't falling; you're flying, floating above the ground. One person described it as the most peaceful moment of their life. Another said it changed them in a way that made them feel fearless. All of them faced their fears, found their courage, and took their leap.

But what stuck with me most was this: Every person who jumped did so with the help of their tandem partner. Someone who had done it before. Someone who knew what to expect, how to ease their fear, and how to land them safely.

That's the role I'd love to play for you.

I can't take your leap for you, but I can guide you through it. I've walked this road multiple times, and I want to be the steady voice that reminds you:

You're not crazy. You're not alone. You *can* do this.

My leap was much like this process of skydiving. There were moments of doubt and anxiety that almost made me turn back. However, there were also profound moments of acceptance, surrender, and faith that carried me through my most difficult moments. I eventually found myself with my feet dangling out the side of the plane and my courage speaking louder than my fear. I closed my eyes, took a deep breath, and leaped. Initially, I panicked, thinking I was falling, but as soon as I surrendered, I found my bliss. On the other side, there was more freedom, peace, and joy than I had ever experienced in my entire life.

If you're ready to live the beautiful life waiting for you, then let's do this. I'm the voice reminding you that you can do it and that it's worth it. And I'm cheering you on every step of the way.

It's time to leap.

It's time to fly.

PART 1

LISTEN TO YOUR HEART

There's a quiet voice within you that is confident, peaceful, and deeply wise. It may have been drowned out by expectations, fear, or the noise of others' opinions, but it's always been there. It's the part of you that isn't afraid to disappoint others or worry about what they'll think. It knows what you truly want. It's where you connect with your most authentic self, with truth, and with love. It's your heart, and in this section, we begin with the most powerful shift of all: reconnecting with that inner knowing. You'll learn how to quiet the noise around you, return to your inner guidance, and listen to the part of you that already knows the way forward.

CHAPTER 1

OBSTACLES

Everything you've ever wanted is on the other side of fear.
—George Addair

The reason I didn't jump off the cliff that day in Hawaii or even make it to the top wasn't because of something that stopped me externally but rather something that stopped me within. Throughout my life, I've seen time and time again how the obstacles that hold us back aren't the ones outside of us, but the ones within us. They are the ones that cause us to doubt ourselves, hesitate, or give up on a dream altogether because we are so afraid of the unknown. As I peeled back the layers of what was holding me back, I realized there were four main obstacles standing between the life I was living and the life calling me. These were shame, unworthiness, lack of self-trust, and the greatest of them all: fear.

SHAME AND UNWORTHINESS

Shame and unworthiness often go hand in hand. Shame makes it hard for us to be open about who we are, while unworthiness tells us that if we are open, we won't be accepted. For instance, if you feel ashamed about a part of yourself or something you desire, you might hide it, which then reinforces the belief that you're unworthy of love and belonging. Shame and unworthiness keep us stuck in a state of inauthenticity, making us afraid to show our true selves or pursue our desires. For years, this was the case for me. I chose to hide instead of being honest about what I was feeling or even giving myself permission to explore my sexuality without judgment. The shame I carried reinforced the lie that I wasn't enough, just as I was.

My sexuality wasn't the only area where shame and unworthiness surfaced. For me, the feeling of unworthiness or "not being enough" has been one of the hardest struggles of my life. Growing up, I was the perfectionist, the straight-A student, and the "golden child." That reputation followed me into adulthood, creating an unspoken pressure for me to maintain the image of someone who had it all together. This often led me to overwork in an attempt to prove I was enough and seek external validation to feel worthy. I knew my family and many people in my life loved me. Still, it didn't stop that feeling of unworthiness from becoming a hole that felt impossible to fill. These would become two of the hardest obstacles on my journey to embracing my authentic life. I wouldn't be able to overcome my shame and unworthiness until I was ready to fully receive myself. This wasn't an overnight process, but as I began to love myself right where I was and accept what I wanted in life, the walls of shame and unworthiness started to crumble.

LACK OF SELF-TRUST

For the majority of my life, I was known as the indecisive one in my family. I struggled with decisions as small as which shirt to buy at the store and as significant as which major to choose in college. I would often find myself paralyzed by indecision because I believed that there was a "right" and "wrong" choice for every situation. I never wanted to get it wrong. I hated making decisions and often sought others' advice rather than trusting my instincts. This led me to believe that I didn't know what I wanted, and even if I thought I did, I was too afraid to act on it, fearing that I would get it wrong. The thought of making a life-changing decision like ending my marriage and coming out about my sexuality was terrifying. I found myself fluctuating from a place of confidence to a place of panic while trying to navigate this decision. Several thoughts often came up: *Are you sure you're making the right choice? What if this isn't who you are? What if you regret everything?* The weight of it all felt monumental.

Like unworthiness and shame, many of us struggle with self-trust. We often aren't taught how to trust ourselves or listen to our hearts. We live in a world where logical, practical decisions are valued over trusting our inner wisdom. I was also taught in Christian culture that our hearts were deceitful and couldn't be trusted. It took me several years to unlearn this and see the role our hearts play in connecting us to truth, wisdom, and love.

What's crazy is that we all possess one of the most powerful internal guidance systems available to us, yet we often don't know how to utilize it. This guidance system is our intuition. We frequently steer away from relying on this because it requires us to trust in what we can't see, to make decisions that may not always make logical sense, and to walk in faith toward a path that feels unfamiliar or unknown. I'm someone who believes in mentorship or guidance from others, but what we all need even more is the confidence to trust ourselves and make decisions based on the truths nudging at our hearts. Many of us have forgotten how to trust ourselves, and for that reason, we shape our lives to please others instead of building lives that align with who we are and what we genuinely want.

Self-trust is one of the most important keys to living authentically. I had to learn to trust myself in a way I never had before to take my leap and create the life I desired to live.

FEAR

Fear has a way of keeping us small and stuck. It can seep into our lives through the experiences we have growing up, the religion we practice, and the voices we hear through the culture that surrounds us. It's less common in our culture to see people living fearless, courageous lives and more common to see people playing it safe and living by the rules. We're often reminded of the risks more than the rewards. For that reason, we settle for ordinary lives instead of extraordinary ones. Fear was my Achilles heel, the weight on my feet trying to pull me down while my heart was trying to soar.

I was terrified of making the wrong decision and ruining my life.

I was afraid of what I might lose or have to give up.

I deeply feared disappointing others, being judged, and not being accepted for who I was.

I was scared of the unknown and the possibility of ending up alone.

But more than anything,

I was afraid to embrace the truth I already knew in my heart because doing so might mean my entire life would have to change.

Most of us grow up with a template for success: attend college, get a stable 9-to-5 job, marry someone of the opposite sex, buy a house, and start a family. It's a beautiful path for some, but what if you want something different? I'd always dreamed big and envisioned my life differently. Still, I didn't realize how much I was following this expected path. Choosing another direction felt uncertain and terrifying, but something inside of me knew there was more for me. To find it, I would have to confront the fears that had shaped my life for far too long: not being accepted, not doing what was expected, not being successful, or not being good enough. I carried many other insecurities, but fear underlay most of them. While my fears weren't my only obstacle, they would be one of the biggest I'd have to overcome on the way to my leap.

FACE TO FACE

On my journey to taking my leap of faith, I would have to face all of these obstacles. I would have to decide whether to continue forward in what I knew to be true or allow fear, shame, unworthiness, and a lack of self-trust to hold me back. Here's what I discovered: When we decide to pursue our authentic life, we will begin walking a path that not only addresses but also heals these places within us that have tried to keep us small and inauthentic for so long. When we come face to face with the obstacles that have tried to hold us back and start to believe that we are more than they've made us out to be, then we will find the confidence to step out on the ledge and take our leap.

My encouragement to you is to put it all on the table. Are you afraid? I was, too! Do you feel unworthy of a beautiful life? I get it. Do you doubt that you can really have everything you're dreaming of? I understand. You are not alone. If you're waiting for all of this to disappear before you take your leap, you will be waiting a lifetime. I'm sharing my obstacles to remind you that while your fears, insecurities, and doubts are valid, they do not have to define your life. Your obstacles will always tell you why you shouldn't start, why it feels too risky, or why it doesn't make sense on paper, but if you're willing to trust your heart and step out in faith, even the greatest obstacles don't stand a chance.

A Thought to Consider

How has shame, unworthiness, lack of self-trust, or fear held you back from the life you desire to live?

PRACTICAL APPLICATION

A Practice for Letting Go

If you'd like to take this a step further, grab a sheet of paper and write down the obstacle(s) that have held you back the most. Now ball up the sheet, hold it in your hands, and tell your obstacle(s),

It's time for me to live the life I desire and be the person I know I can be.

I don't need you anymore.

I'm ready to let go of everything that's tried to hold me back.

I'm ready to start a new path.

I'm ready to be free.

Now, let the paper go. Set it on fire, throw it into the trash, toss it across the room, or imagine yourself symbolically throwing it into the ocean, allowing the waves to take it far away.

You are more than the obstacles that have stood in your way.

You deserve to experience the life that's been waiting for you.

It's your time.

CHAPTER 2

HONESTY

The path is…Deep honesty. Radical acceptance.
Continual surrender. And unconditional love.
—Danielle Bongiorno

I was sitting at the kitchen table with the soft morning light seeping through the windows. I opened my journal to a blank page, with a warm cup of Earl Grey tea beside me. I was reflecting deeply on where I was in life and what I wanted. Tears came unexpectedly as the weight of the truth hit me. What I wanted more than anything was to be real and to stop hiding the parts of myself that I was scared others might reject and just be honest for once, without holding back because of what someone else might think. With this level of honesty came deep fears as well. *What if being honest would cause me to lose my marriage? What if people couldn't accept the real me? What if my honesty cost me everything?* It felt like there was so much risk in being honest, but there was even more risk in continuing to live my life in fear.

One of the hardest people to be honest with is ourselves. I realized this as I wrestled with what I wanted for my life. Honesty meant facing truths I had been avoiding—truths about how I felt in my marriage, what I really wanted in a relationship, and the quiet longings in my heart that I had been too afraid to admit. But honesty became the foundation of my entire process. Honesty was the first step to freedom. I learned that when we're completely honest with ourselves, we not only uncover what we want but also what's been holding us back from the life we're meant to live.

In some areas of my life, I always knew what I wanted. I knew I wanted to play basketball in college, and I knew in my heart that one day I would become a writer and a speaker, but in other areas of my life, I wasn't so sure. Or maybe I was simply afraid to admit it.

I grew up in a religious paradigm that taught me to believe that asking the question, *What do I want?* was selfish and somehow not aligned with God's will. For a long time, I felt like admitting what I wanted, even to myself, was wrong. As I wrestled with this belief, I started to ask myself, *What if my dreams and deepest desires aren't in conflict with God? What if God or the Universe placed those dreams and desires in my heart for me to find the courage to pursue them?* This shift began to change everything.

I realized that when I live connected to my heart, I'm also living connected to God and to Love. Living from this place isn't selfish; it's authentic. It is how we align with the purpose we were created for. This understanding freed me to dream in a way I never had before. I stopped seeing my desires as something I had to fight against and started seeing them as something I was being invited to embrace. As I began exploring what it would feel like to release my fear and live free, I started asking myself these questions:

What do I want?

How big can I dream?

How would I approach my life if fear wasn't holding me back?

Joseph Nguyen says it best, "Whenever we ask questions, answers *always* arise".[2] My heart and mind were opening to new possibilities and a new path for my life—a path where I embrace who I am, express myself authentically, and walk out my life's purpose. However, I was also beginning to realize what was holding me back for so long was the fear of what this would cost me.

During this season of life, I signed up for a course called A New Reality that was designed to help people release the past and start a new, expansive chapter in their lives. I entered the course open-hearted and eager for clarity. On the first day, we did an exercise where we wrote a vision of the person we wanted to become. I sat with a notebook and pen in hand, tapping into my heart. I chose to be completely honest without holding back, and my truth began to effortlessly make its way onto the page:

> I no longer settle in any area of my life. I go after my dreams with my whole heart. I finally let go of the fear of disappointing others and the weight of not being enough. I've stepped into the real me. I feel confident in my own skin. I embrace Danielle. I love her fully. I am ready to take bold steps of faith toward my purpose and live the life of my dreams.

As I read those words back, chill bumps lined my arms, and something shifted inside of me. I could *see* her—the fearless Danielle. She was bold, courageous, and authentic. She didn't settle. She was the true me, waiting to be realized. If I wanted a different life, I had to embrace a different version of myself. Not "more," not "better," just someone willing to be honest about who I really was and what I really wanted.

At the time, I wasn't ready to make big decisions about my marriage or to publicly share the truth about my sexuality, but I could take one small step. I could be honest with myself. I know how scary it can be to be honest. Honesty often requires action. It's hard to be truthful with ourselves and then carry on like nothing happened. At the same time, honesty is often the first step to the freedom, fulfillment, and joy that our heart craves. The moment I began to be honest with myself was the moment my life began to change.

The question, *What do I want?* became an anchor for me during my process. On days when I would question my steps or start to feel that self-doubt rise within me, I would come back to the truth my heart was speaking when I answered. I would begin to see that future me again and believe she was worth fighting for.

PRACTICAL APPLICATION

Now, it's your turn. Grab a journal or a piece of paper and a pen.

Take a breath and ask yourself this question. Respond with what immediately comes to mind and try not to hold back:

What do you want?

I know this question can feel overwhelming at first, but remember, don't hold back or think too much about it. Allow yourself to be real and put it out there. There's no one to judge you or anyone to worry about disappointing. It's just you.

If you want to take it a step further, maybe ask yourself another question:

Who would I need to become to live out this vision?

Would you be someone more confident? Less concerned with what others think? Unafraid to take risks? Take a breath, close your eyes, and let the truth flow.

You don't need all the answers today. What matters is daring to ask yourself what your heart really wants.

Honesty is the first step to creating your authentic life.

CHAPTER 3

EGO AND INTUITION

Intuition is the whisper of the soul.
—*Jiddu Krishnamurti*

I stepped off the stage after a public speaking event, and the chatter immediately started in my mind. *Why did you say that? You spoke too fast. You should have left that part out. What will they think of you now that they know your story?* I felt like I did a great job, but my inner voice was trying to convince me otherwise. Has this ever happened to you? Maybe you're doing something you've never done before, in a situation with new people, or simply trying to decide what to wear on a Monday. Yet, you can't seem to escape the constant chatter that makes you question or doubt yourself. That voice? It's often the ego.

For years, I thought this was just who I was—an overthinker. However, I came to realize that we all have a voice within us that loves to add commentary to our lives and becomes especially persistent and vocal when we take steps outside of our comfort zone or pursue something new. My ego immediately came onto the scene when I tried to take steps forward on this journey. I was met with a range of thoughts and questions that seemed logical but also made me question what I was doing and whether I had what it took to pursue the new path I was beginning to envision.

According to *The Holistic Psychologist*, "The ego is the 'I.' It is how you see yourself. It is the part of your mind that identifies with traits, beliefs, and habits".[3] The one thing our ego resists most is change. So, when we try to make shifts in our lives, our ego starts to speak up. In many ways, it's simply trying to protect us and keep us safe, but more often than not, it keeps us stagnant and prevents us from reaching our full potential. Our ego often triggers fear or doubt, but it does it in the most subtle ways, through thoughts and questions that sound logical and reasonable. Here are a few examples of how the ego speaks:

What if I made the wrong choice?

What will people think?

What if I fail?

I can't do this. I can't handle this.

I'm not good enough.

I don't think I'm ready. I need more time.

What if this doesn't work out?

I'm behind. Everyone's further along than me.

Our ego sounds a lot like our own voice. It blends seamlessly with our normal thought patterns, making it difficult to identify. It's skilled at convincing us that its perspective is the only reality. Before we know it, we're unconsciously repeating the same patterns in our relationships, habits, and life situations because we've mistaken the voice of the ego for the voice of truth.

Once I began to understand how the ego operates, I was able to recognize when my insecurities were becoming obstacles to my progress. Instead of interpreting fear, doubt, or unworthiness as signs that I was on the wrong path or incapable, I began to view them for what they were: attempts by the ego to pull me back into a place of comfort and safety. I started to understand that resistance didn't necessarily mean I was on the wrong path; it simply meant I was stepping into something unfamiliar and new.

There is another part of us that leans into faith instead of fear. It's the part that helped me move through resistance and keep stepping forward, even when my ego's voice was loud and persistent. That part is our intuition. Our intuition is like our internal GPS, guiding us and showing us the way of our highest self. For me, it's a deep knowing that doesn't always make sense in my mind but feels right in my body. When my intuition speaks or nudges me in a direction, it's accompanied by a feeling of peace, calm, and assurance. Hearing our intuition isn't something we force or think our way into. It's something we feel, trust, and surrender to.

I can still vividly remember one of the first times I trusted and acted on my intuition. It was my senior year of high school. I was pursuing my dream of playing college basketball and traveling to camps and tournaments across the country, hoping to be offered a scholarship. In the last tournament of the season, I suffered a season-ending injury. I thought my dream was over until I was invited to visit a small Division II school in North Carolina called Lenoir-Rhyne University.

Before my mom and I were about to head home, the head coach walked up to me and offered me a full scholarship to play for them. I was just off my crutches and still rehabbing my knee, but they took a chance on me. I was thrilled and ready to jump at the opportunity, but he wouldn't let me make a decision on the spot. He told me to go home and think about it overnight, then give him a call.

I'll be honest. Lenoir-Rhyne wasn't on my bingo card when I started my recruiting process. I had always dreamed of attending a larger school, but I loved everything about my visit and the potential to make an impact in an already successful program. Still, I was wondering if I should wait and see if any other offers came through during my senior year. I remember how I felt the whole ride home: excited but nervous. I looked out the window as the trees flew by me and contemplated what felt right for me. There was one other school I was holding out on, knowing they were still interested, but my intuition was telling me to go for it and commit to Lenoir-Rhyne.

I called the coach the next day and enthusiastically told him I was ready to be a Bear. When I got off the call, I walked into the living room with a big smile on my face to tell my parents, and the movie *Hoosiers* was on the TV. I looked at the screen and noticed the name on the front of the kid's jersey. It read, "Hickory," which just so happened to be the name of the city where Lenoir-Rhyne was located. Talk about a God-wink and a little nudge to remind me that I could trust myself and my intuition. My time at Lenoir-Rhyne wasn't easy at first, but it ultimately became one of the best experiences of my life and a chapter for which I will forever be grateful. Now, over 10 years later, I was invited to trust my intuition again and make one of the hardest decisions of my life.

Learning to distinguish between the voice of my ego and the voice of my intuition has been one of the greatest breakthroughs of my life. However, it wasn't something that happened overnight. I needed a practice to help me connect to my body and hone the skill of listening to my intuition. I needed something I could return to again and again as I navigated this journey and prepared to take my leap. In the next chapter, I'll dive deeper into this practice to help you recognize and trust your own inner guidance. But for now, below is a quick guide to help you begin differentiating between the two voices in your life.

Remember, our ego wants us to stay in our comfort zone because it feels safe, but abundant, beautiful lives aren't built there. They are built when we take courageous steps toward what we know is right and true for us. Resistance doesn't mean you've made the wrong choice; it simply means your mind is adjusting to this new path you've chosen. Have faith in yourself and keep moving forward.

Ego	Intuition
Feels tight, constrictive, and anxious	Feels expansive, free, and light
Often comes with fearful or doubtful thoughts	Brings a sense of peace and calm
Creates a sense of urgency, pressure, or self-protection	Often feels aligned with your core self and values. Pressure is off
Can be loud and demanding, filled with "what ifs" and "shoulds"	Comes as a quiet knowing or gentle nudge, without the need for logical validation

The next time you're on the verge of a significant decision or trying to determine which path to take, I encourage you to revisit this table. Ask yourself, *Is this my ego, or is this my intuition speaking?* One will feel tight, constrictive, and anxious, while the other will feel expansive, light, and free.

Trust that you know when your intuition speaks to you.

CHAPTER 4

STILLNESS

Stillness is the pathway to peace.
Stillness is the pathway to wholeness.
Stillness is the pathway to knowing oneself.
Stillness is the pathway to trusting oneself.
Stillness is the pathway to loving oneself.
Stillness is the pathway to joy.
Stillness is the pathway to freedom.
Stillness is the pathway to being who we truly are.
Stillness is the journey that leads us home.
—Danielle Bongiorno

When you are facing a life-altering decision, the temptation will be to listen to every voice and opinion besides your own. I did this for most of my life. I dreaded decisions because I was so afraid of "getting it wrong" and didn't believe I knew what was best for me. However, I knew that deciding whether or not to continue in my marriage was a decision only I could make. I would have to take a different approach than I had in the past and learn how to trust myself.

I started by getting off social media because the constant stream of opinions on how to live your life felt overwhelming. I stopped discussing the situation with my family, even though I am incredibly close to them and rely on their support. I knew I needed to make this decision without carrying the worry or concern about how my choice might affect them. I also knew the people-pleaser in me would come out, and even the well-meaning thoughts and opinions of my loved ones may have swayed me from what I actually wanted. For once, I had to make the decision solely for myself.

This approach became a foundational lesson for me during this season. I learned that whenever you're making a major life decision, considering a different path, or pursuing a new goal, it's often best to keep your circle small and the voices few. Not everyone will understand your path or your decisions. Sometimes, when we share our plans with friends or family, they voice opinions, even when we don't ask for them. Sharing your journey with others before you're ready can lead to unwanted input that leaves you confused or discouraged. The temptation may be to alter your course to appease others or doubt yourself because of the reaction you receive from people you love and trust.

If you're someone who dreams big or wants to pursue a nontraditional path, remember that most people won't share your vision. Instead of belief, they may speak doubt. Instead of faith, they may carry fear. Be cautious about taking advice from those who haven't walked your path or aren't open-minded enough to see different possibilities in life. The quickest way to kill momentum is to surround yourself with people who don't share your vision.

I learned that to find your authentic path, you must tune out distractions. I spoke with one or two trusted people and a therapist during this season, but that was all. Outside of that, I blocked out the noise.

Then...

I got still.

I got still, and I listened to my heart.

When I say heart, I am not just referring to the physical space in the middle of our chest. I am referring to the place within us where we connect to our truest, most authentic selves. It is the place where we discover we are one with the Divine and where we have unlimited access to love, peace, and truth. Our hearts are beautiful spaces where we can come home to our truest selves while also connecting to something so much greater. When we learn to listen to it, we begin to navigate life in an entirely new way.

I can be a very logical and practical person, but some choices in life can't be made with our rational minds; they must be made with our hearts. Don't get me wrong, logic and practicality would eventually come into play as I reached a point where I was ready to take steps forward, and plans had to be made. But initially, it wouldn't be what I needed to make this decision. This decision would require me to feel rather than think my way forward.

Stillness isn't just about slowing down our bodies. It's about giving our minds the space to settle, reconnecting with our hearts, and returning home to ourselves. When I say, "Come back home," I mean finding that place of deep authenticity within, the space where there's no striving, no proving, and no pressure to be anyone other than who we genuinely are. It's a place of ease and contentment. For me, this is the place I find when I am still and connected to the truest part of me.

I began practicing stillness every day during this season. I would go into my room, close the door, and find a comfortable spot on the floor. I'd sit cross-legged with my eyes closed and a small pillow behind me. I'd then take a few deep breaths, place my hands on my heart, and just be. My mind would race with thoughts, questions, and fears, but as I breathed and felt the beating of my heart, peace and stillness would begin to break through like the sun peeking over the horizon on a new day. I started to discover a place of calm within myself where the chatter disappeared and I could hear my heart. My heart knew the way; I just needed to give it space to speak.

I took a writing workshop with one of my favorite authors, Yung Pueblo, during this season. We did an exercise where he gave us a series of questions and encouraged us to write down whatever came to mind. One of the questions he gave us was, "What is your heart saying right now?" This question resonated deeply with me. I took this question into my stillness practice and began asking myself, ***Heart, what are you saying today?***

Sometimes, the response would be simple:

"Trust yourself. Everything will work out."

I tried not to overthink it. I would simply jot down in my journal whatever I felt my heart was speaking:

"This is freedom. Standing in your truth. Accepting who you are and walking with joy and confidence. It's just the beginning of beautiful things."

It was also through stillness that I began to trust my intuition. Your heart and intuition are two very important components when seeking to embrace your authenticity and find the right path. Your heart will reveal your feelings and your true wants and desires, while your intuition will show you which direction to go and will gently tell you "yes" or "no." My heart and intuition would rarely tell me exactly what to do, but would give me the encouragement and nudge I needed to walk out what I already knew to be true. Our answers are already within us, just waiting for us to slow down enough to realize them.

Instead of coming into this place of stillness demanding answers about which path I should take, I would come open-hearted and willing to listen. Instead of asking, *Should I do this or that?* I'd ask myself again,

Heart, what are you saying today?

Truth and a deep knowing would rise above the noise. I would feel the peace that comes from being present in my body and aligned with my true self. I started to recognize that when my heart or intuition was speaking, I would feel a sense of calm and peace. When my ego was talking, I would feel a sense of urgency or pressure. Peace became my guide.

As I continued my stillness practice and began to listen to my heart, I started to feel and know which direction was right for me. I may not have known the full path or how everything would play out, but I knew what step to take next. I had to trust that if I took one step, the next would be revealed to me. Through honesty and stillness, truth and clarity began to reveal themselves.

I realized that what my heart desired was to be in a relationship with a woman. I knew that continuing in a marriage with a man wouldn't allow me to express myself fully and be who I was. I didn't necessarily feel the need to label my sexuality or orientation, but I did need to embrace this truth and allow myself the freedom to fully express myself in my relationships. It wasn't an "aha" moment or sudden epiphany; it was a steady unveiling, a gentle uncovering. It was something I had known deep down for a very long time, but only now was I ready to accept and embrace it. I believe this is how many of us uncover our authenticity and our path. It's already within us, patiently waiting, but we must reach a point where we are ready to hear it, receive it, and step into it.

It wasn't until I started listening to my inner voice above my fear and the expectations of others that I found my truth. What I came to realize is this: Often, our fear screams while our truth whispers. We find our truth as we reconnect to ourselves, our bodies, and our hearts.

Realizing and accepting that I wasn't being true to myself in my marriage and that I was in love with a woman was the first domino to fall for me. This set in motion a yearning for authenticity in every area of my life. When I took the time to be still and listen to my heart about my career, I realized that I wanted to pursue a path more in alignment with my purpose and my passions. Specifically, I wanted to write books, speak, and inspire others. When I thought about my future, I envisioned traveling with the person I love, experiencing new adventures, building wealth, and living a life of abundance. Everything started to become so clear.

This wasn't a practice that I used once and then moved on from. It was a practice that became a lifeline for me in that season and one I still rely on very much today. As we continue with the story, I will share the various obstacles that arose as I attempted to take steps forward. When these moments hit, I often returned to my stillness practice. Here, I would anchor in my truth again and find a sense of peace when the road seemed uncertain.

The key to pursuing your authentic path is to find the voice of truth within you. There will always be voices, both external and internal, that cause us to doubt our path, feel discouraged, or question if we're on the right track. There will also be the voice of our ego trying to pull us back into a place of comfort and familiarity. Stillness helps us cut through the noise and reconnect with our true voice—our deep inner knowing. Time and time again, throughout this journey and even now in my life, I remind myself to trust this voice above the noise. I get still, connect to my heart, and find my true north again.

Stillness led me to the truths of my heart, unlocked the guidance of my intuition, and gave me the confidence to keep moving forward despite any doubts or fears.

Stillness can do the same for you.

———

I want to be honest with you. Learning how to be still did not happen overnight. I remember my very first attempt at "stillness" in college. A friend encouraged me to sit in silence for just 30 seconds. I thought, *That's easy. Of course, I can do that.* I was wrong. I barely made it 10 seconds before my mind started bouncing around like crazy. Don't be discouraged if this is where you start. I would have cultivated this place within me much sooner if I had known then what I know now. The good news is that I plan to share some of these lessons with you.

For many of us, stillness is difficult because we haven't learned how to be with ourselves without distractions. Often, this struggle is tied to a dysregulated nervous system, meaning our bodies are not in a state of calm and rest. Practices such as mindfulness, breathwork, and intentional movement can help cultivate more balance and presence in our lives, making it easier to be still and turn inward. Below are a few of my favorite practices for regulating the nervous system and accessing a state of stillness.

Keep in mind that the goal isn't to get an answer; it's to reconnect to yourself and the present moment. Here, you will find your peace and truth. Be kind to yourself as you begin this process. Focus on discovery, not perfection. Release the pressure and enjoy!

INTENTIONAL BREATHING

Our breath is one of the most powerful, underutilized tools in our bodies. Dr. Nicole LePera, better known as The Holistic Psychologist, explains that when we focus on a long exhale, it helps activate the parasympathetic nervous system (rest and digest). A simple yet effective way to regulate the nervous system and cultivate a sense of peace in the body is through intentional breathing. Place one hand on your belly and one hand on your heart. Breathe in deeply through the belly for a count of three. Exhale for a count of six. Spending extra time on your exhalation helps slow your heart rate and shift into a calm, balanced state[4].

MINDFULNESS

Mindfulness is the simple act of being present in the moment. One of my favorite teachers of mindfulness is the wise Thich Nhat Hanh. In his book *You Are Here*, he offers a few simple phrases to anchor us in the now.

"As you breathe in you can say to yourself, 'Breathing in, I know that I am breathing in.'"

"As you breathe out, you can gently say, 'Breathing out, I know that I am breathing out'".[5]

He offers an even simpler version:

"Breathing in, I am here. Breathing out, I am here".

When I catch my mind in a thought spiral, I will begin whispering this under my breath. You can do this practice while driving, walking, or doing dishes. It's not something confined to sitting on a meditation mat; it's a tool that is available whenever you need it.

MOVEMENT

The practice of yoga taught me the connection between movement and stillness. During one class, an instructor shared something that transformed my perspective. He said the entire purpose of the physical practice of yoga—the sweat, the poses, the effort—is to prepare for Savasana (corpse pose). It gets you to a place where you can bypass your thoughts and simply be.

With this in mind, I started using movement as a tool to find my stillness. One way I like to do this is by rolling out my mat and allowing my body to move freely. Sometimes, this resembles a yoga flow; other times, it involves stretching what feels tight or simply moving in a way that feels right for my body. Eventually, I'll reach a point where I can settle onto the mat and just be. When we approach movement in this way, it can serve as a gateway to stillness and a deeper connection to our hearts.

NATURE

Nature has an incredible way of slowing me down and reminding me that everything is taken care of. I love to sit on my back porch, surrounded by nature, and take in the sights and sounds around me: the wind blowing through the trees, the creek trickling in the distance, and the birds chirping as they fly from tree to tree. When I take in this scene, I'm reminded that nature never worries or strains; it just is. It doesn't try. It knows that it will be taken care of, and it simply exists. When I step into nature, I remind myself that I, too, can live in this flow and state of trust. Nature always has a beautiful way of pulling me out of my head and back into my body, into a place of stillness and a state of peace.

A great way to combine the benefits of movement with nature is to take a leisurely walk outside without a phone. Allow yourself to be in the present moment, release what's on your mind, and soak in the beauty of your surroundings.

Initially, stillness can feel overwhelming and impossible to access, but with practice, we can all find this place of peace within us. Try these various tools and practices to help balance your nervous system and guide you into a state of stillness. Some may work for you, and some may not. That's okay! Find what works for you and keep it a part of your routine. Remember, stillness isn't just reserved for sitting on a meditation mat; it's a practice we can develop within ourselves every moment of every day.

PRACTICAL APPLICATION

An Exercise to Practice Stillness and Listen to Your Heart

1. Close your eyes and take three slow, intentional breaths, inhaling through the nose and exhaling through the mouth.

2. If you hear your mind rumbling, try saying this while taking each breath:

   Breathing in, I know that I am breathing in.

   Breathing out, I know that I am breathing out.

3. Notice when you begin to feel a space of stillness in your heart, mind, or body.

4. Once you feel settled, place your hands on your heart and ask yourself, *Heart, what are you saying today?*

5. Remember, when your heart speaks, it often feels calm, gentle, and peaceful.

6. Write down whatever comes up without judgment. It may be a word, a sentence, or just a feeling. Trust that you know the voice of your heart.

7. Don't feel the need to force anything. If all you do is sit and breathe, this is more than enough. The point of the entire practice is to connect to yourself and begin trusting that you can hear your heart speak.

8. Stay in this space for as long as you need.

PART 2

EMBRACE YOUR FAITH

Taking a leap isn't about knowing how everything will play out; it's about trusting yourself to walk forward, even when the path ahead is unclear. Faith is more than a feel-good word; it's the strength that helps you continue forward when the fear is loud, the doubts are heavy, and the anxiety is consuming. In this part, you'll learn how to develop an unshakable faith to overcome your fear and trust the process, even on your hardest days.

CHAPTER 5

TRUST

"Your heart knows the way. Run in that direction."
−Rumi

The pain shot through my knee as I collapsed to the floor. I couldn't stand up on my own. This was when I knew that something was very wrong. I saw my mom out of the corner of my eye, running from the bleachers down to the court. The pain was excruciating, but what was even worse was the thought that immediately came into my mind: *I think I just tore my ACL.*

I came home from my basketball tournament and went straight to the doctor. After a few tests, he confirmed my fears, and reality began sinking in. *What would this mean for my basketball career? Would I still be able to play in college? Was I going to miss my entire senior year?* The weight of it all felt crushing.

I cried my fair share of tears and wrestled with endless "whys." I couldn't understand why this happened to me, especially at such a pivotal time, when I was so close to attaining my goals. Ultimately, I reached a point of acceptance and realized that there was only so much I could control. I had done everything in my power to shape my future in basketball, but I couldn't stop this injury from happening. I couldn't change the fact that my knee was hurt or that I would have to miss my entire senior season of high school basketball. All I could control was my approach forward. Rather than staying stuck in the past or fixating on regrets, I made a radical decision: I chose to trust. I decided to believe that things would still work out, my dreams weren't over, and somehow, this setback could become something meaningful. And through that experience, I learned the power of trust for the first time.

At the time, the only way I understood trust was through my faith in God. I believed that someone greater than me was in control, guiding my path. This belief gave me a sense of peace and confidence that I wouldn't have had if I had relied solely on my own strength. While I still hold this perspective, I now see trust as a universal language that transcends any single religion or belief system. To me, trust is acknowledging and accepting that we don't have full control and that there are greater forces at work in the universe guiding and supporting us along our path. Trust is also about doing what we can and controlling what we can while letting go and inviting divine forces to make a way.

I played my part by completing my knee rehab and emailing my highlight clip to schools, but at the end of the day, the rest was out of my hands. I had to trust that it would all work out for me and that a school would find me. Sure enough, Lenoir-Rhyne was the one school that responded to my email and offered me a full scholarship even though they had never seen me play. I knew my actions played a role, but I fully believe it was my decision to trust that allowed everything to work out for me when the road seemed bleak.

This experience taught me two important lessons: how to trust in a higher power guiding my path and how to trust the process when the future seems uncertain. I would need both of these as I made choices to create an authentic life, but I would need another form of trust even more: the power of trusting myself.

Trusting myself was something I was still learning to do. I had spent so much of my life trusting others over myself. I even had someone very close to me tell me multiple times that they knew me better than I knew myself. These beliefs ran deep. *Could I really trust myself? Did I know what was best for me?* I had given away my power, and I knew I'd have to reclaim it to take my leap.

I also had to trust that even if my decision didn't go as planned or didn't unfold the way I expected, it didn't mean I had made the wrong choice. The journey of self-trust isn't about getting it "right." It's about discovering yourself and learning to make choices that align with who you are and the life you feel inspired to create.

One of the simplest ways I began to develop self-trust during this season was by making small decisions without seeking advice or validation from others. I practiced turning inward first and asking myself what I wanted before looking outward for input. Whenever fear or anxiety crept in, even over small decisions, I reminded myself again and again: *It's not about right or wrong. It's about learning to trust myself.* I also made it a point to have fun with the process and enjoy the journey of discovering who I was, what I preferred, and what I wanted. The truth I came to understand was this: You learn to trust your authentic voice by taking steps of faith and going for it.

I still recall a day during this process when I was second-guessing myself and deeply struggling to trust. My doubts weighed heavily on my mind, and I questioned everything that had brought me to this place. I turned to a meditation practice I had used years before, where you visualize meeting your future self on the beach. I envisioned the future me; she was beautiful and glowing. She radiated confidence and carried a sureness in who she was. Her joy was undeniable. We were both standing near the shore, with the waves crashing in and washing up toward our feet. I walked toward her with my head down and told her honestly about the doubts filling my heart and mind.

She listened patiently, then placed her hand over my heart and said, "Trust this. Your mind will lead you in so many different directions, but your heart knows the way."

These words became my anthem: ***My heart knows the way.***

When she spoke those words, a calm washed over me. It was the same calm I felt in moments of stillness when the nudges of my intuition became clear. I knew the road ahead wouldn't be easy, but that day, I found a greater confidence to trust myself and move forward in the truth of what my heart was speaking. I was reminded once again that my thoughts couldn't be my source of truth in this season. I would have to trust my heart.

———

If I needed any more reassurance that I could trust my path, I found it 30,000 feet in the air on a work trip. I brought along a book I had recently stumbled upon: *Untamed* by Glennon Doyle. I hadn't heard of it before, but it didn't take long for me to see stark similarities between Glennon's journey and my own. She was on her own path of authenticity and self-discovery, vulnerably sharing her experience of being married to a man for many years and eventually finding herself in a new, beautiful relationship with a woman for the first time.

I clung to every word as I read. I deeply connected to her story, her questions, and her moments of breakthrough. There's a part where she describes meeting her partner for the first time. As I read her description of this encounter, chill bumps lined my arms. Tears welled up in my eyes, and a deep longing rose from within: *I want that.* I could barely put the book down at this point. My heart felt such a deep connection to her story and the truth she was uncovering. It gave me the courage I needed to pursue my own authentic path.

I continued reading on the flight back home and came to another part where Glennon and her partner spent time alone for the first time. It was tender and intimate. My heart knew, deeply and undeniably, that this was the life I wanted for myself. This time, the tears didn't just well up in my eyes; they fell hard. I had an entire moment on the plane, sobbing into my shirt, trying to dab the snot dripping down my nose with my sleeves because I didn't have a tissue. People probably thought something was seriously wrong, but I didn't care. The truth of my heart was sinking in even more and reminding me that I could trust my heart and my path.

When you are following your heart and the path that is right for you, there will be moments of confirmation that anchor your truth even deeper. This was one of those moments for me. It will give you the confidence to keep moving forward and to trust yourself. It will silence the voices of fear and remind you to continue following the voice that matters most: your heart.

I was in a yoga class one night, and the session was coming to a close. Beads of sweat were dripping down my face and arms as I lay on my back for Savasana. I closed my eyes while the soft music played and found myself drifting into a vision. In my mind's eye, I saw a river gently flowing, lined by two banks covered with lush grass and green trees. Then, I saw myself in a canoe, floating effortlessly down the river. I wasn't paddling; I was simply allowing the flow of the water to carry me. A sense of ease and surrender washed over me. I thought, *This is what it feels like to trust instead of controlling and worrying.*

I was on the cusp of making one of the most significant decisions of my life and was feeling the weight of it all with every step. As I saw myself gently floating down the river, I was reminded of what happens when we let go and trust. Peace began to fill my body and ease my mind. I didn't know exactly where the canoe was headed or how everything would play out, but I knew I could trust the path my heart was calling me to.

Trust is a choice we make to lean into the unknown and believe in something greater, whether that *something* is the wisdom of our heart, the guidance of the universe, or a divine plan. Trust is what allows us to step into the canoe, let go of the paddle, and let the river take us where we are supposed to go.

As you pursue your own authentic path, remember that the canoe is always available to you, divine love is supporting you, and flow happens when we step into alignment with our truest selves. Place your paddle down and allow the current to take you where you're meant to be.

Your heart knows the way.

CHAPTER 6

ANXIETY

*I think and think and think, I've thought myself out of happiness one
million times, but never once into it.*
—Jonathan Safran Foer

I woke up in the middle of the night with my mind racing. The
house was silent, but my thoughts filled the space with noise. I
tried to close my eyes and go back to sleep, but my thoughts continued to run rampant like a tornado destroying everything in its path.
I glanced at my phone. It was only 4 a.m., but I felt as if I had been
awake for hours. I tossed and turned for what seemed like an eternity, trying to find a sense of peace.

I experienced numerous mornings like these as I took steps toward
what my heart was calling me to. I would wake up in the middle of
the night or before my alarm, feeling heavy and questioning every
decision that had led me to this point. It was so intense at times that
I'm not even sure how I managed to get through that period. I believed I was making choices that honored the woman I wanted to be,
but my anxiety made me feel otherwise.

In many ways, it felt like everything was falling apart. What I
didn't realize at the time was that this unraveling was completely
normal when making life-changing decisions. Change often triggers anxiety, not because something is wrong, but because the mind
craves certainty. Even though I had found peace in what I wanted, I
was still learning how to move through the discomfort of choosing a

new path. My mind kept trying to analyze and overthink each step, but that only made me feel more anxious and stuck. It wasn't until I learned how to create space between myself and my thoughts and come back to the present moment that I finally began to feel free.

My anxious thoughts also took a turn when I discovered the book *Don't Believe Everything You Think* by Joseph Nguyen. In this book, Joseph explains that "the root cause of our suffering is our own thinking".[6] He differentiates between thoughts and thinking. Thoughts are something we have, while thinking is something we do. Take, for example, clouds in the sky. When a thought pops into our minds, it is like a cloud appearing in the sky; we notice it, and it whisks away. Thinking, however, is when we fixate on the cloud—we dwell on it, we start to worry if it's going to be a rain cloud, we wonder if storms are in the distance, we stress that bad weather is coming, and then we begin to think about the plants on the front porch that might get blown away by the wind and our dog who gets stressed out by storms. One little thought has evolved into a full-blown storm of overthinking, leaving us feeling anxious and unsettled.

Understanding this distinction didn't erase my anxiety overnight, but it made me more aware. When anxious thoughts arose about my situation, my choices, or the future, I would try to become aware of them and stop myself from spiraling into a storm of thinking. In anxious moments, I reminded myself, *I am not my thoughts. Peace is found in the present moment.* I took a few deep breaths, felt my feet on the ground, and shifted my focus back to the here and now. I also leaned on practical tools to manage the anxiety in my body, such as going for a walk, practicing gratitude, or utilizing simple tapping exercises (shared below).

When doubts and fears weighed heavily on my mind, I paused and recognized that I was thinking rather than living in the moment. One of my favorite teachers on mindfulness, Thich Nhat Hanh, says it best: "Life is only available in the present moment." Anxiety took hold when my thoughts pulled me into the past or dragged me into the future; peace returned when I brought myself back to the present.

Our ego and anxious thoughts often work together when we step into the unfamiliar. The key is to give yourself grace and remember this: You are not your thoughts. When you feel overwhelmed, pause, take a breath, and watch them float by. Return to your truth and find your peace.

One of the ways I returned to my truth was by asking myself a simple question: *What do you know?* Another way to frame it is this: *What is one thing you can control?* Anxious thoughts will always fixate on the unknown or the worst-case scenario, but truth and peace are found in the present. They lie in what we *do* know.

I knew I was following my heart.

I knew there was more for me than the life I was currently living.

I knew I had moments when I felt confident in my decision, and in those moments, I also felt at peace.

Once again, peace became my guide.

Instead of spiraling into uncertainty, I rooted myself in what I knew to be true.

I share this part of my process to be honest with you about my struggles and to remind you that you're not alone. Anxiety may try to derail you on the path to a new chapter, but don't be discouraged. Pause if you feel overwhelmed. If you need support, seek it. Therapy was helpful for me during this time, and I highly recommend it if you need a safe outlet to process your emotions. Remember to be mindful of whose voices you allow in, as too many opinions can amplify anxiety.

Anxiety is real, but it is also conquerable. Despite what it tells you, your truth is stronger.

Breathe, trust, and take the next step forward.

PRACTICAL APPLICATION

I mentioned I used some practical tools to help manage anxiety during that season. Below are a few of my favorite practices for when I feel ungrounded or overwhelmed.

COLD EXPOSURE

The vagus nerve, which activates the parasympathetic nervous system (and helps calm us down), starts at the base of the brain and extends to every organ in the body. To help ease anxiety, place a cold pack or a bag of frozen vegetables on the back of your neck for 1-2 minutes while breathing slowly and deeply. As you do this, notice your body calming and your anxious thoughts settling.[7]

BOX BREATHING

This is one of the most well-known breathing exercises for calming the nervous system. It's very simple and effective and can be done almost anywhere, at any time. This is one of my go-to breathing exercises whenever I feel anxious or need help calming down before going to sleep.

  Place one hand on your belly to remind yourself to breathe from there during the practice.

  Inhale slowly for 4 seconds, hold for 4 seconds, slowly exhale for 4 seconds, and hold for 4 seconds.

  Repeat this cycle for a few rounds until you feel grounded and calm.[8]

EARTHING OR "GROUNDING"

"Earthing (also known as grounding) refers to the discovery that bodily contact with the Earth's natural electric charge stabilizes the physiology at the deepest levels, reduces inflammation, pain, and stress, improves blood flow, energy, and sleep, and generates greater well-being".[9]

How I practice: I like to stand in the sun with my bare feet on the earth, close my eyes, place both hands on my heart, and take deep breaths to ground myself. I also enjoy grounding by walking barefoot on the beach. Even just 10 minutes of grounding can begin to reduce stress and anxiety.

EMOTIONAL FREEDOM TECHNIQUE—"TAPPING"

Tapping is a simple yet powerful technique for relieving stress and anxiety. One effective spot to tap is the Gamut point, which is believed to help calm repetitive thoughts, obsessive thinking, and worry. Below is a step-by-step guide to tapping this point.

Start with a deep breath: Inhale deeply through your nose, then exhale slowly through your mouth. Take a moment to center yourself.

Tap the gamut point: The Gamut point is located on the back of either hand, in the indentation between the knuckles of the ring finger and little finger, about half an inch down from the knuckles. Gently tap on the gamut point with your other hand's fingers

Breathe and focus: While tapping the Gamut point, inhale deeply, hold for a moment, and then exhale fully. Allow yourself to breathe slowly and naturally.

Repeat the affirmation: As you continue tapping, repeat the affirmation to yourself, either silently or out loud: "I am safe." Allow the words to resonate with you.

Optional—Add more affirmations: After a few cycles of tapping, you can add variations of the affirmation, such as the following:

"I am grounded."

"I am at peace."

Finish with a deep breath: Once you feel more centered, take another deep breath to close the practice.[10]

Breathe

When you don't know what to do.
When you feel overwhelmed.
When up seems down and down seems up.
When you feel defeated and question if you have what it takes to continue.
When you need to find yourself again.
When the weight of the world feels too heavy.
When your thoughts become consuming.
When your mind gets the best of you.
When you can't find the energy to take another step…
Breathe.
Let your breath bring you home.
Bring you back,
To truth,
To love,
To peace,
And to joy.
All you need is already within you.
Allow your breath to guide you home.
And remind you who you are.
Fully loved.
Completely whole.
More than enough, just as you are.
When you don't know what else to do,
Just Breathe.

CHAPTER 7

FEAR

Death is not the biggest fear we have; our biggest fear is taking the risk to be alive—the risk to be alive and express what we really are.
—Don Miguel Ruiz

F ear is like the scary monster lurking under the bed. Deep down, we know there's no monster there, but when we're kids, it's easy for our minds to create that scenario. We work ourselves up by imagining what it looks like and fearing what might happen if we step off the bed and place our feet on the floor. The fear takes over so much that we forget a simple truth: If we just turn on the light, we'll see there was nothing to be afraid of all along.

I don't use this analogy to diminish fear. Our fears are valid and can feel very real, but sometimes, we just need to turn the light on so we can see what's there. I remember fearing what people would think or say about me if I ended my marriage and started a new relationship with a woman. I recall fearing that I would disappoint my parents or let them down if I chose a nontraditional path. I remember the fear and anxiety I felt about having my needs met if I stepped away from a stable career to pursue my dreams. Those feelings were real and scary, but they were also an invitation to turn on the light and see the truth. They were an invitation to grow, discover myself, and heal. Over time, I realized fear wasn't something to run away from but rather something to explore.

The key isn't to suppress fear or pretend it doesn't exist. It's to acknowledge it, accept it, and explore where it's coming from. When we seek the truth behind our fears, we allow ourselves to quiet those wild thoughts and regain our power.

I also discovered that fear likes to create worst-case scenarios in our minds. Every time I tried to take a step forward, the same set of fearful thoughts would come running. *What if I get this wrong? What if it doesn't work out? What if I lose everything?* Each of these questions pointed to a deeper fear: fear of failure, fear of loss, and fear of not being enough. They were rooted in different life experiences that became the stories my mind told me whenever fear surfaced.

One of my fear stories resurfaced when I started writing my book. *What if I give my all to something only for it to end in disappointment or failure?* Maybe that fear took hold when I tore my ACL and watched my dreams flash before my eyes, or perhaps it took root even earlier, in a moment I can't quite remember. Either way, it no longer served me to continue believing it. I was beginning to see all the ways fear had tried to dictate the story of my life, and I was ready to write a new script.

Our fear stories don't just disappear on their own. They'll continue to replay in our minds unless we make a conscious decision to choose new thoughts and beliefs. This requires us to meet that fearful part of ourselves with compassion while replacing the old fear-based narrative with a new, faith-filled one.

One way I rewrote my script was by asking different questions:

What if it turns out even better than I can imagine?

What if it all works out?

What if I experience everything I desire and more?

I started replacing fearful thoughts with faith-filled ones. It didn't happen overnight, but in time my courage grew. Worst-case scenarios began to give way to best-case scenarios as I started to see a path forward that wasn't defined by fear.

As powerful as this was, I realized that shifting my thoughts was only part of the equation. Fear wasn't just a thought in my mind; it was physically present in my body. I was able to take an even bigger step toward freedom when I learned how to release the fear I was carrying in my nervous system.

Fear, in its most basic sense, is a survival response. It's our body's intelligent way of protecting us from real or perceived threats. I started to notice throughout this process that I didn't just *think* fearful thoughts; I *felt* fear in my body when I tried to take steps forward. My chest would feel tight, my heart would speed up, or a knot would form in my gut. Often, our past experiences or trauma cause us to hold emotions like fear in our bodies and nervous systems. Dr. Bessel van der Kolk describes this phenomenon in his book *The Body Keeps the Score*, explaining that trauma is not just a psychological experience but also a physical one. The body retains memories of traumatic events and stores unresolved emotions in the nervous system.[11]

My body had been carrying fear from different traumas and life experiences. There are five main responses to trauma: fight, flight, freeze, fawn, and flop[12].

My body's response to a "threat" typically defaulted to freeze. I would freeze when I tried making decisions because something about decisions felt life-threatening to me. Throughout my life, even small choices, such as picking a shirt or selecting a gift, could trigger a freeze response. I was so afraid of getting it wrong or messing up that even small decisions would feel monumental in my nervous system. You can only imagine how intense this trigger felt when it came to a decision as big as ending my marriage and revealing a new side of myself to the world. The thought of starting a new life and walking a path I had never walked before triggered every part of me that craved predictability and control. It also triggered every fear about whether I would still be accepted or loved.

Looking back, I can see that my childhood experiences, including two life-threatening illnesses at a young age, might have contributed to the fear I was carrying in my body. There could have been other experiences I went through as a child that I don't even remember or even things passed on to me at birth. Rather than trying to pinpoint every source of fear, I learned that what mattered most was allowing myself to *feel* it so I could finally *release* it. We all carry trauma. It's less important to understand what caused it and more important to feel and release the trapped emotions that have lingered from those experiences and are affecting the trajectory of our lives.

One day, I was standing in the kitchen, thinking about my situation, when I felt fear rising in my body. I was so tired of fear calling the shots in my life. I felt an intuitive nudge to start bouncing very lightly. I allowed my knees to bend and my arms to hang loosely. As I bounced, I envisioned the fear falling off my body into the earth. At the time, I didn't know that bouncing activates the parasympathetic nervous system, which is the part of our body responsible for calming us down. All I knew was that it felt like what I needed at that moment. While I was bouncing and literally shaking this fear off of me, I felt an unexpected desire to let out a scream. I opened my mouth and yelled, "AHHHHHH!" As soon as the sound left my body, tears started falling. I was telling my fear that it couldn't control me any longer. It felt empowering and freeing, so I did it again. I bounced, cried, shook, and let my fear go. As crazy as this moment probably looked, it was exactly what I needed to release what was holding me back and keeping me from moving forward.

A few weeks after this, I had another moment on my back porch where I felt myself being pulled to release my fear again. I started practicing yoga but then felt led to try a technique I had learned called nonlinear movement. Essentially, this practice involves putting your hands and knees on a mat and moving your body in nonlinear circles or movements. This practice, created by Michaela Boehm, is powerful for releasing stored emotions. I started moving my hips in circles one way, then switching directions. As I continued to move and really press into the circles, I felt this agonizing ache inside of me. It was a deep desire again to release my fear and be free. Everything in nature moves in curves, spirals, and waves; nothing is linear. It's humans who have forced things into boxes, straight lines, and rigid structures. And here I was, in the middle of my backyard, pressing into those circles, reclaiming the truest parts of me.

I knew fear was what had been holding me back for so long. The fear of disappointing others, of getting it wrong, or being viewed as anything less than perfect. Fear was that mountain standing between who I was and who I knew I could be. I moved and felt the fear that was gripping my hips, and slowly started to let go. I kept moving until I felt myself softening. Eventually, I found myself sitting cross-legged on the mat with my heart facing the woods in my backyard. I closed my eyes and took a deep breath.

A quote from Yung Pueblo came to my mind: "I held my fear by the hand, honored its existence, and thanked it for teaching me that happiness exists beyond the boundaries it creates."

So I did just that. I repeated this quote like a prayer, honoring my fear while also releasing it. Fear helped me survive some life-threatening situations early in life, but I was no longer interested in just surviving. My soul was begging to thrive. It was time for us to part ways so I could live the abundant life waiting for me.

I placed my balled-up fists on my knees, turned my hands over, opened them, and let it go. I knew something within me had changed. I felt lighter, softer, and more at peace. I had just taken another step toward the woman I was meant to be.

For a long time, I thought my goal was to *eliminate* fear. But I've come to realize that fear, much like the ego, is simply trying to protect us. Deep down, there's a younger version of me who just wants to feel safe, loved, and secure.

When fear rises now, instead of fighting it, I acknowledge it. I remind myself:

You're safe.

You can't get it wrong.

Life is about learning and growing, not being perfect.

You are more than enough.

I practiced replacing fear-based thoughts with truth-based thoughts, like the ones above. I met the part of me that was afraid and reminded her it was safe to move forward and create a new life on her terms.

When we take steps in life toward something new or something we've never done before, fear inevitably arises. That's its job. But fear isn't here to decide our future; it's just here to keep us in the familiar. The truth is that our nervous system doesn't care whether something is good or bad for us; it only craves what it already knows.

It will cling to a familiar struggle over an unfamiliar freedom every single time. So, instead of trying to banish fear, what if we got curious? What if we asked, *Is this fear protecting me from real danger, or is it simply guiding me to the edge of something I've never experienced before?* Here, we get to decide whether we will allow fear to keep calling the shots or thank it for teaching us that happiness exists beyond the boundaries it has tried to create.

You may never completely get rid of your fear, but you can release its hold on you. You can choose to move forward despite it. You can build a life defined by your courage, not your fear. And when you find yourself standing on the edge, contemplating your next leap, you have a choice: You can let fear keep you where you've always been, or open your hands, let it go, and leap into the life you've always wanted.

PRACTICAL APPLICATION

When fear takes hold in your body, it's a sign that your nervous system has shifted into fight-or-flight mode and is seeking to regulate itself. I've shared several practices throughout this book that can help, but here are a few more exercises to calm your nervous system and release fear.

SHAKING AND BOUNCING

Just like I did in my kitchen that day, shaking or bouncing can help release built-up fear and anxiety, bringing your nervous system back into balance. Let your limbs hang loose, gently bounce your knees, or shake your body. Do this for a few minutes while taking deep breaths. Continue until you feel a sense of release.

SWAYING OR ROCKING

Gentle swaying or rocking can help reset your nervous system and bring a sense of ease. I like to sit cross-legged on the floor and slowly rock side to side or back and forth, allowing my body to self-soothe.

COREGULATION WITH A PARTNER

If you have a partner or loved one, try this simple yet powerful practice from Dr. Nicole LePera:

1. Sit or stand facing each other.

2. Place your hand on their heart while they place theirs on yours.

3. Focus on deep belly breathing.

Your nervous systems will naturally begin to sync, helping both of you feel more grounded and balanced.[13]

EMOTIONAL RELEASE

Sometimes, the most effective way to release fear is by allowing yourself to feel. After practicing any of the techniques above, you may notice emotions rising to the surface. If you feel the urge to cry, let it flow. Crying is a natural way to process emotions and return to a state of emotional regulation. Rather than resisting it, allow yourself to surrender to whatever needs to be released.

CHAPTER 8

FAITH

Leap, and the net will appear.
—John Burroughs

I was 8 years old, lying on our white and blue plaid 90s couch, battling a near-fatal illness, when I had my first encounter with faith. Beside me sat one of the dearest people in my heart, my Mema. She was a Holy Spirit-filled, Jesus-loving woman who often spoke of angels and the golden streets of heaven as though she had already walked them. Her unwavering faith made it easy to believe in things unseen.

I remember my Mema asking me if I believed that Jesus loved me. I told her, "Yes." She then asked if I wanted Him to live in my heart and be with me forever. That sounded good to me, so I said yes again. We prayed a simple prayer together. No fancy words or religious jargon were needed, just faith—a child-like faith that didn't need to know all of the reasons why or the answers but simply believed.

Years later, I learned that during my illness, my Mema said a simple prayer over me daily that went something like this: "She will not die; instead, she will live to tell what the Lord has done." I believe her unwavering faith, as well as the faith of many others, helped me through that season of my life. I went on to live, and I carry a deep conviction in my heart that I am here for a purpose and that my life matters. I never take a single day for granted, knowing that the breath in my lungs is a gift.

My story had a happy ending, but I know this is not the case for everyone during a difficult time. There are times when we feel we've had great faith, yet things don't go as planned. This is the mysterious and sometimes difficult aspect of faith. What I do know is that I've seen the power of faith in my life, and I know it's real. The fact that I am here today and have overcome all that I have is my reminder of how powerful it can be.

Faith is a deep sense of belief and confidence in what cannot be seen. Faith is the decision to view the future through the eyes of the heart rather than the physical ones. Faith says, "I don't fully know how, but I know it will." Faith bridges the gap between the physical and the transcendent, pulling visions down from the unseen and transforming them into reality. It allows us to hold onto something greater while remaining grounded in the present moment. Faith also reminds us to take life one step at a time. And with each step, another one reveals itself. Ultimately, faith is the decision to believe in miracles and possibility. Without faith, I could not have taken my leap.

———

One morning during my journaling practice, I closed my eyes and saw a vision of three roads. The first road continued straight, representing the familiar path I'd been walking—a path built on comfort and habit. To the right, I saw another road marked by logic and reasoning, paved with "shoulds" and what seemed like the "right" way to go. But to the left was a different road, an unfamiliar one. A path illuminated by faith. I knew this was the road I was being called to walk; it was a path not built on logic or what I thought I "should" do, but rather, a completely new one built on faith.

Faith's partner is belief. The two go hand in hand, reminding us that if we can keep the vision in our hearts and refuse to give up, we will eventually take hold of what we're seeking. Belief came naturally to me as a child. I dreamed of playing college basketball at Duke University and going to the WNBA. I was often the smallest player on the court, but my belief never wavered. If anything, it motivated me even more to defy the odds and make my dreams a reality. I knew what I wanted and believed I could achieve it, no matter what stood in my path. I still carried this faith into my adulthood but sometimes found it harder to believe with this same tenacity.

As we grow older, maintaining our beliefs can become more challenging because we become increasingly aware of our insecurities, weaknesses, and the obstacles we will face in achieving our goals. But time and time again, life has shown me that those who believe in themselves and in their dreams are the ones who create extraordinary lives.

On my journey toward authenticity, faith and belief became very challenging at times. I began carrying a vision in my heart for a future life that felt so out of reach at times, but I knew this was the path I was being invited to walk. When I decided what I wanted for my life and the future I wanted to create, I began taking steps forward in faith, and I would eventually have to take my leap.

I felt so deeply in my heart that something beautiful was on the other side, but I didn't really know. I didn't know what it would be like to be in a relationship with a woman. I didn't know what it would take to write my first book and start a business. I didn't know how I would feel on the other side of divorce. I didn't know how people in my life would react to these major life moves. I had no clue how everything would pan out or if I would end up happy, but I had faith that my heart was leading me to a future I had always wanted. No matter how scary it felt, my faith began to speak louder than my fear, giving me the strength I needed to persevere.

Here's the truth I've come to believe: If you want to create an authentic life or pursue the dreams in your heart, you will need faith. I'm not just talking about fluffy, feel-good, "you can do it" faith. I'm talking about the kind of faith you hold onto when you don't yet see the things you're hoping for. When you're stuck in your doubts and others tell you it's not going to happen or your dreams are too big. The faith that holds onto the vision and inspires you to continue taking steps forward even when you face obstacles. This is the type of faith I'm talking about. It's powerful and beautiful but also gritty and real. This is the faith I grasped during my season of discovering my true self and stepping away from my job, and it's the same faith I cling to now as I write these words and build my dream career.

So, how do you build faith and deepen belief? For me, my faith is strengthened every time I take a step forward despite my fear or doubt and see it work out for me. It builds every time I look back and realize how far I've come. My belief expands when I witness others overcome their challenges and achieve their dreams. It serves as a reminder that I can do it, too. Sometimes, to believe in more for our own lives, we must first see others do it. It's easy to look at someone else's success and feel jealous or think we aren't worthy of the same, but what if we viewed their success as proof that it's possible? If they can do it, so can we. Every time we choose to believe in something greater than what we've previously believed, we break through our limits and create space to receive even more.

Building faith and deepening belief can also happen in subtle ways throughout our day-to day lives. As I continued on my path, I began to notice signs and synchronicities that seemed too meaningful to be mere coincidences. These little nudges from the Universe also came at the exact right time, reminding me that I was on the right path.

As cliché as it sounds, I began seeing specific numbers, particularly the combination 222. These numbers would appear on street signs, clocks, or license plates. I'm the type who immediately pulls out my phone and asks Google for the meaning. One explanation said, "Trust that everything is working out exactly as it's supposed to, with Divine blessings for everyone involved. Let go and have faith".[14]

As crazy as it may seem, the Universe will speak to us through many different methods, numbers being one of them. I can recall numerous instances throughout my journey where I would begin noticing a sequence or pattern of numbers, and upon looking it up, it was the exact message I needed at the time. I encourage you to keep your eyes open on your own journey and not take repetition as coincidence, but rather a sign to slow down and listen. If you need further convincing that God or the Universe speaks to us through signs, I have a few more stories to share with you.

I live in a suburban neighborhood surrounded by woods and not too far from a river. It's not uncommon to see wildlife like alligators, herons, or turtles, but deer are a rare sight. One morning, as I walked near the pond by my house, I spotted not one but *five* deer across the water. It felt like a God-wink. Naturally, I looked up the meaning, and here's what I discovered:

"Angel number 5 is here to let you know that change is coming… It is a number that works as a symbol of individualism and encourages you to hold firm when it comes to self-belief, freedom, and carving your own journey in life."

Additionally, deer can represent gentleness, love, following your intuition, new beginnings, and divine guidance. "The deer is first and foremost a reminder that you need to listen to your intuition".[15] One article explained the meaning further by saying, "The Deer opens up new horizons for you, whether for a professional or personal project, or for a more important change in your life…It will show you that you have the energy to make a fresh start with even greater vigor and power".[16] Seeing the five deer that day was an undeniable reminder that I could trust my intuition. It was time for change, and I had Divine support behind me as I took steps toward this major life move.

I experienced one more undeniable sign during this process while driving home from a weekend trip. We hit some storms during the first half of the journey. Once the rain cleared and the sun began to come out, we saw not one but three rainbows as we drove the rest of the way home. Of course, I had to look up the meaning again and found this explanation: "If you feel you need to make a change, a rainbow may suggest it's time to take a leap of faith. The arrival of the rainbow delivers a flicker of hope that it's possible".[17] At this point, it felt like so much more than a sign; it felt like confirmation that I was exactly where I was supposed to be. I already knew what my heart was calling me to do, but now I had even more courage to trust myself and take the leap.

Time and time again, I would have moments where a sign would cross my path, encouraging me to keep walking and keep believing. When we choose to walk in faith, signs will follow. They are whispers from the Universe reminding us that we aren't alone and encouraging us to keep pressing forward.

———

I now carry the faith of someone who has taken leaps in life and experienced so much beauty and joy on the other side. Have there been days when I've wanted to give up and go back to what's comfortable? Absolutely! But there have been even more days that are so full of joy, freedom, peace, and everything my heart was wanting and more. I know it's not always easy to find faith and belief, so I am offering you some of mine in the hope that it helps you find the strength to keep moving forward.

You may not know exactly where your path will lead you or what obstacles lie ahead, but if you are following your heart, trusting your intuition, and living true to yourself, I promise you it will be good. I promise that if you hold onto faith and keep believing in the life you want to create, it will happen. Life never goes exactly as planned, but what if it turns out even better? What if it's even greater than you were imagining? This is what I experienced when I took my leap of faith, and this is what you can experience, too.

PRACTICAL APPLICATION

Close your eyes and imagine three roads: a familiar one you've been walking, one of logic, and one of faith.

Which road is your intuition calling you to walk?

Where do you feel this road is leading you?

How can you take one step toward this new path today?

You don't need to know the entire path yet; you just need to take one step of faith and begin to believe.

PART 3

ACCEPT YOUR TRUTH

In this part, you'll learn how to accept your truth with compassion. I know "your truth" is a phrase that's often overused and misunderstood, but I believe it's essential to living an authentic life. Your truth is simply what feels right, real, and aligned for you. This part of the journey will help you release shame, rewrite limiting beliefs, and reconnect with who you are, not by changing yourself but by embracing who you've always been.

CHAPTER 9

REWIRING
BELIEFS

*"There is one grand lie - that we are limited.
The only limits we have are the limits we believe."*
—*Dr. Wayne Dyer*

I glanced at the time on my computer: 10:05 p.m. My eyes were burning from staring at a computer screen all day. It was a Thursday night, and I was still at my desk working. This had become the norm in that season of my life. I was closing deals, proving myself as a dedicated team player when the company needed me most, and making more money than I ever had. Still, I was exhausted, burnt out, and neglecting myself in the process.

I had carried a belief for most of my life that to be successful, you must work hard and give your all. I believed that if you were willing to do a little bit more than everyone else, you'd always come out on top. For years, these beliefs served me well. They made me determined, competitive, and a winner. They helped me strive for greatness both on and off the basketball court and persevere when others gave up. I took these beliefs into my first year at my corporate job, and guess what? I found success again, but I also found myself overworked, in physical pain because I wasn't taking care of my body, stressed, anxious, and exhausted.

My belief that there was only one way to success was driving me into the ground. The reason is that beneath these beliefs was an even deeper one. It was the belief that if I didn't work hard and prove myself, I wouldn't be enough. What I came to realize on my journey was that my beliefs, particularly my subconscious ones, were playing a significant role in creating the life I was experiencing.

Our beliefs are powerful forces shaping our lives. However, the majority of them lie beneath the surface, so we're unaware of just how much they influence our actions and decisions. In fact, only about 5% of our thoughts and beliefs are conscious. That means the other 95%—the ones we're not even aware of—are often the ones directing our lives.[18]

It's important to understand this if we're going to create our authentic lives and consciously choose the path that's best for us. Sometimes, despite our best efforts, we find ourselves stuck in the same place because our subconscious beliefs are holding us back. At other times, we may not even consider new possibilities for our lives because of deeply ingrained beliefs that shape the way we navigate the world. It's not until we're willing to examine these beliefs on a deeper level and begin the work of rewiring the ones that no longer serve us that we can start to accept our truth and walk our authentic path.

When I found myself in a state of burnout (again), I realized this approach no longer served me. I decided to step back and ask myself why I kept finding myself in this situation. It wasn't always burnout. Before my corporate job, it often looked like an injury on the basketball court or simply feeling exhausted all of the time. Whatever the case, it was a clear sign that I didn't know my limits. The first step to rewiring beliefs is *awareness*. I began asking myself simple questions about success, hard work, and rest: *Why do I believe this? Where did these beliefs come from? What do I want to believe instead?*

According to Dr. Nicole LePera, "A belief is a practiced thought grounded in lived experience." Our beliefs begin forming as soon as we exit the womb and are either affirmed or ingrained as we move through life, interact with others, and face various experiences.[19] Most of our beliefs are shaped by our parents or caregivers, but they're also influenced by the people around us during childhood, our education, religion, culture, and the society in which we grow up.

I once heard beliefs described like this: Imagine a mountain covered in snow. Now, picture a path that's been shoveled out and walked over again and again. It's deeply imprinted in the mountain and easy to follow because it's been traveled so many times. That's how our beliefs are formed, through repeated thoughts and experiences that become familiar pathways in our minds. Once a certain way of thinking is established, we often continue down that path without questioning it until something or someone helps us see things from a different perspective.

Now, imagine what it would take to carve a new path in the snow. It would require focus, effort, and repetition. It might not happen overnight, but over time, a new path will begin to take shape. The same is true for rewiring our beliefs. With the right tools, support, and perspective, we can start to create new beliefs that better align with who we are and the life we want to live.

Two tools that helped me go deeper and uncover some of my subconscious beliefs were meditation and visualization. Awareness is a powerful first step, but sometimes we need more to go beyond the conscious mind and access what lies beneath the surface. As I began to see my beliefs more clearly, I started asking myself, *Do these reflect the person I want to be, or is it time to let them go?* I still believed in the value of hard work, but I also wanted to start thinking that rest, balance, and taking breaks could be part of that definition as well. I wanted to believe I could slow down, operate from a place of flow instead of striving, still be successful, and still be enough.

I had to be willing to let go of beliefs I'd carried for many years to make space for new ones to take root. Once I became aware of the stories I held around hard work and success, I started making more intentional choices about how I wanted to live and think. This looked like scheduling a yoga class at 6 p.m. on weekdays to create a clear boundary around my workday. It looked like choosing not to work on weekends and trusting that I would still be successful and close deals.

I began envisioning a new approach to my days and a version of myself that aligned with these beliefs. This version of me set boundaries and took breaks but also closed deals and attracted opportunities with less effort and greater ease. She was still motivated and thriving but no longer stressed and anxious. Her body felt strong and pain free because she was taking care of it, and she wasn't exhausted when the weekends rolled around. Once I could see her, I started showing up as her every day.

As my internal beliefs changed, my external world reflected this change. I practiced living out this belief again and again, shoveling a new pathway in my mind for a new belief to take root.

On my journey of discovering my authentic self and embracing the path that felt right for me, I realized I needed this approach now more than ever. Up until then, I had never really thought about or questioned where my beliefs about sexuality, love, or marriage came from. *Were these my beliefs? Were they my parents'? The religion I grew up in? The culture I was surrounded by?* I had to step back and ask more questions:

Why do I believe what I do?

Is this a belief I want to hold on to?

Does it reflect who I am and who I want to be?

When it came to my journey toward authenticity, I began to open myself up to new perspectives on love and happiness. I realized the shame I carried about my sexuality was rooted in judgment and the belief that being in a relationship with someone of the same sex was wrong. This was a really hard one for me to swallow. I didn't think I was judgmental when it came to this, but the shame I felt told me otherwise. I was reminded that the judgment we feel toward others is usually an inability to accept something within ourselves. As I learned to accept myself and this new belief, it freed me to love in a much greater capacity.

I also believed that love wasn't supposed to be easy and light. Marriage was supposed to be difficult, and growth or transformation was the goal above being happy. I witnessed my parents in a loving marriage growing up, but I still adopted the belief that for anything to be good or worthwhile, it had to be challenging. I was also reminded often in the Christian culture that the point of marriage was sanctification or the process of making one another holy. Again, it felt selfish to want to be happy.

While I still believe growth is essential in a relationship, I have also started to embrace the idea that love can be easy and that it is okay to want to be happy. In fact, happiness and joy are beautiful by-products of a healthy relationship. More than anything, I came to believe and accept the truth that I deserved to be happy and experience an easy, light, out-of-this-world kind of love.

What's important to remember is that our beliefs can change. While we may have grown up believing one thing our entire lives, we have the opportunity to assess whether those beliefs truly represent our authentic selves and how we want to show up in the world. Through awareness and intentional choices, we can begin to think new thoughts and create new beliefs that shape who we are and the life we want to live.

PRACTICAL APPLICATION

Discovering Your Truth Through Rapid Response

One of the most powerful ways to uncover your subconscious beliefs and align with your authentic self is by responding to thought-provoking prompts without overthinking. The goal is to tap into your immediate thoughts and feelings before fear, doubt, or hesitation can take hold. These quick responses often reveal your deeper truths, beliefs, and desires that may be hidden beneath the surface.

As you go through the following statements, take a deep breath, relax, and write down the very first thought or feeling that comes to mind. Don't judge or edit your responses; just allow them to flow naturally. You might be surprised at what you uncover.

Instructions:

For each of the statements below, respond with whatever answer comes to mind (for instance, it could be *Yes, No, Absolutely,* or *I'm not sure*) as quickly as you can. This is not about being "right" or "perfect"; it's about honesty and self-discovery.

- My life is a reflection of my true wants and desires.
- I trust myself to take risks and pursue new things.
- I feel safe expressing my true self to others.
- Fear no longer dictates my decisions.
- My dreams are worth pursuing.
- I am ready to let go of what's holding me back.
- I trust my heart and intuition to guide me.
- I am living in alignment with my purpose.
- I believe I have what it takes to create a beautiful, abundant life.

Reflection Questions

After completing the exercise, ask yourself these questions:

- Were any of my responses surprising?
- Which statement felt easiest to agree with, and why?
- Which statement felt hardest to agree with, and what might that reveal?

By exploring these answers, you'll begin to see patterns and beliefs that can either support or hinder your journey toward authenticity and fulfillment. Use this as an opportunity to lean into what feels true and practice letting go of what doesn't serve you.

CHAPTER 10

SHAME

When we find the courage to share our experiences and the compassion to hear others tell their stories, we force shame out of hiding, and end the silence.
-Brené Brown

I didn't realize how deeply shame had rooted itself in me until the first time I felt an attraction to another woman. I was in college at the time and a leader in a well-known sports ministry on campus. Ironically enough, I met this friend at one of these sports ministry camps. I'll never forget the moment when I realized I had feelings for her. I was terrified to tell anyone and ashamed to even admit it to myself.

I still remember my heart racing when I finally found the courage to confide in a friend about what I was experiencing. I was so afraid that they wouldn't accept me or would think about me differently if I admitted this. My status as a leader in a Christian organization only intensified that fear and shame. I grew up Christian and had experienced everything along the spectrum, from wine and bread during communion at the Episcopal church to dancing in the aisles at the Pentecostal church. While I had come to believe in a God who loved me, I had also been shown time and time again that this part of me was unacceptable.

I saw girls sent home from Christian camps for being gay. I was shown verses that labeled this as sinful and wrong. For a time, I believed it too. How could I not feel shame when these desires came up within me? As Brené Brown says, "Shame is the intensely painful feeling or experience of believing we are flawed and therefore unworthy of acceptance and belonging"[20]. That's exactly how I felt—ashamed, unworthy, and wrong for wanting or even considering something I had been taught to reject.

So, how did I begin to heal this?

I allowed myself to be seen.

I remember the moment my heart was racing as I told my friend I had feelings for another girl. She didn't judge. She didn't reject me. She simply told me she loved me. That was a moment of healing. I remember the moment my mom wrapped her arms around me after a season of hiding and lying about my sexuality. She held me close and told me she loved me no matter what. That was another moment of healing. I've had Christians, people I once feared would judge and condemn me, fully accept and love me for who I am. That was healing, too.

My shame didn't disappear overnight. In fact, it's taken years to release the weight I kept hidden for so long. Even now, I still have moments when I must remind myself to be kind and recognize that I'm still healing. However, each time I've taken a courageous step to be myself or speak my truth, shame has lost a little of its power.

We heal shame by courageously sharing our story and allowing ourselves to be seen. That doesn't mean we unload or share everything with everyone (in fact, it's not recommended). Instead, we start with safe spaces, places where we feel we will be received and accepted. We bring our full selves to the table and allow ourselves to be known. I must reference the brilliant Brené Brown again because she says it best: "If we share our shame story with the wrong person, they can easily become one more piece of flying debris in an already dangerous storm".[21] On the other hand, "If we share our shame story with someone who responds with empathy and understanding, shame can't survive".[22]

No matter who you are or what you've done, you are worthy of love and acceptance. I'm sharing my shame story with you to remind you that you are not alone. I also want to offer a safe space for you to know, without question, that you are enough just as you are.

I see you.

I love you.

You're enough.

PRACTICAL APPLICATION

Find a safe space to share your shame story, and be a safe space for someone else to share theirs.

CHAPTER 11

ACCEPTANCE

In order to have what you really want, you must first be who you really are.
—Tim S. Grover

It was a beautiful Sunday afternoon, and I was taking a walk downtown. I grabbed an iced chai latte and found a spot with a view of the river. It was a warm day, but the breeze that floated up from the water made it almost perfect. I was listening to a podcast on living authentically, a topic that had been central to my life for the past few years. I reflected on the ways I still hid, afraid to fully show who I am, even to those closest to me. For years, I asked myself, *Why can't I fully accept myself?* But I never had an answer. It felt like one of the simplest things to do, yet it was difficult at the same time. Despite how hard it felt, I made a conscious effort to learn how to accept myself. I found moments of breakthrough during meditations or times alone where I started to love myself more fully and let go of the need to be anyone other than who I was. Yet, something was still missing.

Self-acceptance doesn't happen in isolation. Sometimes, it takes being seen and loved by another to fully see and love ourselves. I began to reflect on this new relationship in my life with a woman, the way she made me feel, and how I was changing as I learned to embrace myself more and more. She had a way of loving me that reminded me I was more than enough. Her love empowered me to love myself more fully and to embrace the parts of me I'd kept hidden for so long. She loved the part of me that had felt unlovable and that gave me permission to do the same.

I continued to look out over the water, reflecting on the changes I was beginning to feel in myself. I was becoming clearer not just about who I wanted to be but also about how I wanted to live. I felt a beautiful sense of contentment and flow that morning, the kind that only comes when you are in alignment with your truest self.

These feelings stayed with me as I went inside and unrolled my yoga mat. I turned toward the window so I could feel the sun on my face as I moved through the poses. Music was playing in the background, allowing me to fully step out of my mind and into my body. I reached a point where I was no longer thinking but simply one with the moment. I lifted my leg toward the sky while in downward dog, then brought it to the front of the mat so that I was in a low lunge position. I then lifted my arms straight out above my head and started to rise into a position called "crescent pose."

As I brought my arms over my head, lifted my chest, and stood tall, a deep revelation also rose within me: I am her. This version of myself I had been longing to be all along. The woman in the vision. I realized that I was her. I didn't need to change or work harder to become her; I simply needed to receive her and deeply accept who I already was.

With my arms lifted and my heart open, this realization sank deeper. Tears began streaming down my face. The weight of the moment brought me to my knees. It was as if, in that moment, I saw myself and accepted myself fully for the very first time. I had been searching my whole life for this feeling of "enoughness," and for some reason, on this beautiful Sunday, I felt it deep in my soul. I wasn't searching anymore. I allowed myself to be who I was, fully and completely. I accepted *every* part of me: my attraction to women, my desire to be in a relationship with a woman, the shame I had once felt for wanting it, and the longing to express myself fully and authentically in every area of my life. It was expansive, liberating, and unlike anything I had ever felt before. All I wanted was to sit in that moment and never let the feeling escape.

I lingered for a while longer as the tears continued down my face. I opened up my hands to the window as if I was giving an offering to the world when it hit me. This is the point—to bring our truest, most authentic, vulnerable selves to the world and proclaim:

This is who I am. I embrace myself, I accept myself, and I love myself fully. I am enough.

I'm still trying to put into words what happened that day. It was one of those moments that I will remember forever. It felt as if I was witnessing the real me for the first time in my life. It was a full-body acceptance of Danielle. I saw her, I felt her, I was her, and I was enough. I felt in perfect harmony and a state of flow. I embraced who I was, and I was no longer striving to find her. So often, we think we need to become someone other than ourselves or that there is some grand destination we must reach before we can start living. I came to discover that wasn't the case. The real journey lies in fully accepting and loving who you are right now and living authentically as that person in the world.

I couldn't take steps forward in my journey until I was ready to fully accept the woman I was made to be. If I had moved forward, still seeking to care what other people thought or trying not to disappoint people, I would have set myself up for failure. The truth is, not everyone will agree with the choices you make or the life you decide to live. However, if you know it's right in your heart and you love and accept yourself despite what anyone else thinks, then you've won.

When you decide to be your authentic self and to pursue the path that lights your soul on fire, you will inevitably encounter people who don't understand or agree. But when you carry a conviction in your heart that you are enough and worthy of every good thing your heart desires, nothing can stand in your way. Everything you believe in and dream of will come to fruition as you embrace your truth and walk out who you are.

PRACTICAL APPLICATION

Acceptance Mantra

Take a deep breath and place your hands on your heart.

Repeat these words like a love song to yourself. Speak to the part of yourself who feels unworthy or has never felt like enough:

I see you.

I accept you.

I love you.

You are more than enough.

If you feel led, repeat it a few more times with your eyes closed.

You can also repeat this practice while looking at yourself in the mirror. Or you can speak to the younger version of you who needs to hear these words.

Feel it in every fiber of your being and stay in this moment for as long as you need.

CHAPTER 12

GRIEF AND JOY

It's possible to feel joy and grief at the same time. It's possible to look forward to the horizon while mourning what you've lost.
—Sara Holland

I didn't expect the range of emotions I would feel on this journey. On one hand, I began to deeply grieve a marriage and a life I was leaving behind. On the other hand, my heart was filled with excitement over the life I was beginning to envision for myself. As much as I may have chosen a different path, that didn't take away from the sadness I felt over the one I was leaving behind. I would have to come to terms with letting go of a life I once knew.

I met my former husband when I was 16. A deep bond and friendship had existed long before we became husband and wife. I wasn't just letting go of a husband; I was losing my best friend, and that hurt the most. I had hoped that this friendship might continue, but I also knew in my heart that he might no longer be in my life ever again. I wasn't just grieving what was; I was also grieving the future I thought I was going to live.

It would have been easier to bypass these feelings and focus on what was to come, but I knew that if I didn't allow myself to feel what I needed to feel, I wouldn't be able to fully step into my next chapter. So I cried. I felt the pain of losing someone very close to me and allowed myself to feel as much as I could in order to let go.

Some days, it would hit me unexpectedly. I would see something that reminded me of the relationship, and a weight of sadness would come over me. I remember leaving the house one day and seeing our wedding picture on the wall. I got into my car in the garage, and the tears began to fall. I sat and cried for what felt like an hour, just letting it all go. The memories—the good times and the hard ones—all came bubbling up in my heart. When those moments hit, I would try to honor the feelings, honor that relationship, and allow the grief to pass.

Of course, the doubts crept in on the days when the grief hit hard. I'd ask myself again if this was the right choice and if I was doing the right thing, but what I kept coming back to during these hard moments were the realizations I had found in my moments of stillness—the times when I allowed my heart to speak and found peace in which direction to go.

The truth is, even before I was married, there were moments when I questioned if this was truly the path meant for me. Yet, despite my hesitations, I wasn't ready to trust myself or the intuitive nudges urging me to listen. I convinced myself—time and time again—that this was the right path because everything seemed "right." In the end, I made the best decision I could with the understanding I had at that time in my life.

I didn't regret the choice I made, but I knew I could no longer ignore my truth. Had I stayed in my marriage for my husband's sake, I would have eventually realized that I had abandoned myself. If I wasn't choosing myself, I wasn't loving myself. And we can't fully love others until we first learn to love ourselves.

I remember one day standing in the kitchen and envisioning having a daughter down the road. I thought about what I would say to her if I had stayed and continued on the path I was on. I knew I wouldn't be able to look her in the eyes and truthfully say this was the life I wanted for myself. However, what I would like to tell her is this: "Don't be afraid to follow your heart and go after your dreams. Your heart knows the way."

I wasn't walking away from a "bad" marriage; that's what made this even harder. Most people saw our marriage and probably thought it was perfect. It can be even harder to walk away from something good because you will continue justifying all the reasons why you should stay. However, just because something appears good doesn't mean it's right for you.

I began to ask myself, *What if there is more waiting for me? What if I can't even begin to know how amazing my life can be because I don't have a frame of reference for it?* I simply had to trust and believe that where my heart was leading was worth pursuing.

On the other side of this sadness, I started to see the hope for something beautiful. I was beginning to find myself in a way I had never experienced before, and I also found love with another person that was unlike anything I had ever felt before. It was a love that felt so right, so good, so freeing, and so true. When I was with her, everything seemed to fall into place, and nothing else mattered. Laughter was always present when we were together, and we could be completely content doing nothing at all. As cheesy as it sounds, when we were together, time stood still. We could be riding in the car, running errands and listening to music we both loved, or taking a walk by the river. It really didn't matter; any time we were together, things just felt easy and right. I would get lost in her eyes. Her touch had a way of reminding me that everything would be okay, and her presence brought out the softest and most genuine parts of me. She made me feel like I could do anything and made me want to dream bigger than I had ever dreamed before. I never had to be anything other than who I was, and in this love, my heart began to find a home.

At the time, I didn't really know what was to come of this relationship. There was still so much to figure out and walk through, but my heart kept telling me that there was something beautiful here. And I knew it was worth pushing through every bit of discomfort or challenge to see what would be on the other side. The love I was experiencing with her was something I had always wanted but had honestly counted myself out from having. My heart began to believe that this type of love was possible for me.

Major life transitions, such as divorce, can easily bring feelings of guilt or shame, but remembering this helped me extend grace to myself: There are seasons for everything in life. Even when we choose to move on or make a change, we can still carry gratitude for what that season brought into our lives. Over time, I came to accept that my marriage wasn't a failure just because it ended in divorce. I chose to trust that it served its purpose, and I still hold gratitude for that relationship and that chapter of my life.

If you're on a journey of becoming someone new or stepping into a new chapter, you will experience both grief and joy. In some instances, we have to grieve a version of ourselves that we are leaving behind. In others, we must grieve relationships, jobs, or chapters of life that are ending so that we can step into what's next. At the same time, there is hope, excitement, and anticipation for what's to come. It can be hard to hold two emotions at once, but it's a necessary step when you decide to take a leap of faith. My reminder to you is not to be surprised when grief hits. In fact, I encourage you to embrace it. It's okay to feel sadness over a chapter, a relationship, or a life that's ending, even if you choose to exit or start a new path. It's also okay to experience a mix of emotions, such as sadness, joy, and excitement, all at the same time. Feel what you need to feel and know that it's all accepted on this journey.

———

I sat on the beach with my toes buried in the sand and the salty breeze brushing against my face. Not far off, I noticed a sandcastle. It was tall and intricate, clearly the result of someone's time and care. I watched as the tide began to rise and the waves crept closer, eventually reaching the castle. Little by little, the edges softened, the walls started to collapse, and the ocean slowly pulled it back in.

Just a little further down the beach, my eyes caught sight of two children laughing as they worked together to build a new sandcastle. There were smiles on their faces and joy surrounding them as they filled buckets with sand and built their masterpiece.

I kept looking back and forth. One moment held grief. The other held joy. One was about letting go. The other was about beginning again. And somehow, they both existed in the same place at the same time.

At that moment, the beach became a metaphor for my journey. Just like the castle being washed away, I was learning to let go of what was while feeling joy for what was on the horizon. This didn't take away from the castle that was built. The memories of the experience were still there, but just like the tide, which comes and goes, our choices clear the way for something new to begin.

The waves weren't only taking something away; they were also clearing room for something new to be created. On the other side of grief, there is always the possibility of a new beginning—if we're brave enough to let go, trust the process, and rebuild.

PRACTICAL APPLICATION

Tools for Navigating Grief and Joy

Allow Time for Reflection: Set aside intentional time to sit with your emotions. Maybe light a candle, grab a blanket, and journal. Or take a walk in nature, away from the distractions of life. Use this time to honor your feelings without judgment.

Gratitude Journaling: Write down what you're grateful for from the chapter you're leaving behind, as well as what you're looking forward to in the chapter ahead. This helps balance grief with hope.

Create a Ritual of Release: Letting go can feel more tangible with a ritual. You might write a letter to the person, relationship, or life you're grieving, then ceremonially release it—burn it, bury it, or toss it when you feel ready.

Find Anchors of Joy: Identify small practices that spark joy or hope in your day-to-day life, such as playing a favorite song, meditating, or connecting with supportive loved ones. These can help you find balance on heavier days.

Mantra or Affirmation Practice: Choose a mantra that resonates with you, such as "I allow myself to feel everything I need to feel" or "I trust the process of letting go and becoming my most authentic self." Repeat it daily to ground yourself.

- **Seek Support:** Grief and transformation can be difficult to navigate alone. Whether through a trusted friend, therapist, or support group, lean on others who can listen without judgment.

- **Celebrate Small Wins:** Even in the midst of grief, find moments to celebrate your courage and the steps you're taking toward a new chapter. Acknowledge your progress, no matter how small.

PART 4

PURSUE YOUR PATH

In this final part, you'll begin turning clarity into action. You may not know how the entire path will unfold, but you'll be ready to take the step, or even the leap, toward the life your heart has been quietly calling you to. Your courage will speak louder than your fear, and you'll carry a deeper confidence in who you are and what you want. This part is about honoring what's true, trusting what you've uncovered, and pursuing your most authentic, abundant life.

CHAPTER 13

COURAGE

*Life bends for the courageous, and courageous is what you're being called
to be. You're already facing the right direction — the only thing left to do
is leap.*
—Rebecca Campbell

I still remember my hands shaking and my heart racing as I sat
across from my husband on the couch, preparing to tell him I
wanted a divorce. While we both knew this was likely where our
path was headed, it felt surreal to actually say the words out loud. I
thought to myself, *This is it. I'm really doing this.* As hard as that moment was, I knew deep down that I couldn't stay. I looked him in the
eyes and told him, and myself again, that I wouldn't be living true to
myself if I stayed. I was finally taking the leap to honor the truth I
had discovered in my heart. I was ready to let go of everything that
had tried to hold me back, embrace my wings, and fly.

Just days before, I came across a quote by Alana Fairchild that
struck me deeply: "You have the wings to fly. Sometimes, we don't
realize it until we leap over the edge of what we have known and
begin to soar into a new life".[23] Courage was my wings, reminding
me that when I jumped, I had to trust I would soar into a new life.
I couldn't see it all yet, but faith assured me it was out there waiting
for me, and my heart told me it was time.

This wouldn't be my only leap, nor would it be the only time I'd
need courage as I continued to move forward. Eventually, I told my

parents and family about my decision, and months later, I came out publicly for the first time. Each step was terrifying, but my courage kept reminding me that I could do it. I carried that same strength with me as I took bold steps to build my dream career. I left a successful, six-figure job to pursue my lifelong dream of writing my first book—the one you're holding in your hands. I tried to write a book in my twenties and pumped out about 70,000 words, but I never finished it. When I left my job and took the courageous leap to try again, I wrote the first draft of my book in just 7 weeks. With each leap, my courage grew, and the conviction that I could create the life I wanted began to take hold. I realized I wasn't stuck or tethered to a life that no longer served me. I was courageous, bold, and free to soar.

I knew I needed courage to take my leap, but what I didn't realize was that this resolve had always existed within me. It started when I stepped back onto the basketball court after an 8-month recovery from my ACL injury. It grew when I left a comfortable and familiar coaching job to step into an unfamiliar sales role. My courage became stronger when I admitted to another woman, for the first time, that I had feelings for her. It deepened even further when I asked myself this simple but life-changing question: *What do you want?* When you get honest with yourself about what you want and the life you desire, you'll find that courage is already there, just waiting for you to take hold of it.

My courage continued to grow as I learned to listen to my heart and separate the voice of fear and ego from the voice of truth and faith. I felt my courage take shape every time I chose myself and the life I wanted to live. It grew stronger as I trusted my intuition and began taking steps of faith to honor those inner nudges. And through deep acceptance, I unlocked the courage and confidence to be my most authentic self. My courage had always been there, simply waiting for me to embrace it.

None of us lacks courage. It's available within all of us, waiting for us to grasp it and pursue the life we desire. So, I'll ask you: **What leap is your heart calling you to take?** Maybe it's a decision you've been wrestling with, a truth you've been afraid to voice, or a dream you've put on hold. You can continue to think about it and talk about it, or you can take the leap. Trust that you already have the courage. It's been within you all along, just waiting for you to say "yes."

What are you waiting for?

Bold, Courageous, and Free

She trusts herself,

She goes after what she wants,

She no longer questions if she's right or wrong.

She's bold, she's courageous, she's free.

She released the need for approval,

She doesn't follow the path of expectations,

She walks a new path guided by the desires in her heart.

She's bold, she's courageous, she's free.

She chooses a life that feels good to her soul,

She's unafraid to make mistakes,

She knows she's living in her authenticity and truth.

She's bold, she's courageous, she's free.

CHAPTER 14

SURRENDER

The moment of surrender is not when life ends. It's when it begins.
—Marianne Williamson

What they don't tell you about leaping is that, initially, it can feel like you're falling. I felt a rush of freedom and joy when I finally took my leap of faith. The decision was made, the words were spoken, and the life I wanted was in motion, but not long after, a surge of anxiety and fear came over me again. For a moment, it didn't feel like I was flying. It felt like I was falling—plummeting to the earth without anything to hold me. I called it my "freak-out moment." It's the one that no one warns you about—the moment right before the chute deploys. It was my last attempt to hold onto a sense of control and cling to what was left of a life I was choosing to walk away from.

My first real lesson in surrender came during my freshman season of college basketball. I poured everything I had into becoming the player I wanted to be that year, but despite my efforts, I still struggled on the court. My confidence wavered, and my adjustment to a new coaching style was harder than I'd anticipated. By the end of the season, I was questioning whether I even wanted to continue playing the game I'd loved my entire life.

That summer, I was invited to be a leader at a camp in Georgia for high school athletes. Traveling to Georgia to work at a camp for teenagers wasn't exactly what I had planned. After the challenging year I'd had on the court, I felt like I needed to be in the gym every day, refining my skills and regaining my confidence. However, deep down, something told me it might be good to step away from the game for a little while and shift my focus, so I decided to give it a try.

Before I continue this story, I want to pause and provide some context. As you've probably noticed throughout this book, my relationship with God and Christianity has evolved over the years. I've had experiences that I'm deeply grateful for and others that've left scars. It's taken time to work through it all and rediscover God through a lens of love. I understand how the mention of Christianity or Jesus can be triggering, because it once was for me, especially as I navigated embracing my sexuality.

Over time, I've been able to release the beliefs that no longer served me and find appreciation for the moments when I encountered something deeply spiritual. I believe that true surrender is spiritual, and you don't have to follow any particular belief system to experience it. Moments like the one I'm about to share can happen simply by opening your heart to the possibility that there is a divine source of energy and love surrounding us all.

The camp I attended was a Christian-based camp, so on the very first night, before the campers arrived, we gathered for a worship service. I'll never forget walking into the sanctuary and seeing a joyful, larger-than-life man standing behind a keyboard, singing with a soulful energy that filled the entire room. Midway through the service, he played a gospel song that I'll never forget called "I Give Myself Away." He invited us into a moment of surrender—a moment to release whatever weights we had been carrying so we could be fully present for the week ahead.

As the keys played, it was as if something inside me took over. Before I knew it, I was at the front of the church, kneeling with my hands by my side and tears streaming down my face. It was one of those *"How did I get here?"* type of moments. The weight of my difficult freshman season was hitting me, and the pressure I felt to excel and not fail rose to the surface once again. At that moment, I decided to let go. I surrendered my basketball career to God and released my grip on what I thought was supposed to happen, as well as what I desperately wanted to happen. I stopped fighting and striving and opened myself to the limitless possibilities that God (or the Universe) might have in store for me.

I began to realize that my reason for being at Lenoir-Rhyne and on this earth was far greater than just basketball. It was a moment I will never forget. It set the tone for the rest of my basketball career and, honestly, the rest of my life.

I carried that moment of surrender into my next season on the court. I had always thought that success meant becoming a starter, scoring 20 points a game, and earning All-Conference honors, but maybe success at this level would look different for me. When I let go of the expectations I had for myself and the small plan I had envisioned, I discovered a new path and an even greater purpose for my time there.

I realized that what my team needed most was a steady, reliable point guard, as well as a strong leader. Leaning into that role allowed me to grow in ways I hadn't expected. Eventually, I became a 2-year captain and starting point guard. I helped lead us to a Conference Championship and a #1 ranking in the national tournament. More importantly, I became the type of teammate who left a positive, lasting impact. When I surrendered the idea of the player I thought I was supposed to be, I became the leader my team needed. I also discovered a version of success far more meaningful than anything I had previously imagined.

That lesson on surrender has stayed with me ever since. Surrender isn't about giving up; it's about opening up to new possibilities. It's about releasing control so opportunities and blessings can enter your life and trusting that a divine source of love is guiding and supporting you every step of the way.

When I took my leap of faith, I had to surrender all over again. As much as I wanted to hold onto the illusion of control, I ultimately had to let go of the plane and just go for it. I had to believe that the chute would deploy, the free fall wouldn't last forever, and most importantly, that I wasn't falling. I was flying!

I found that surrender wasn't a one-time act but a practice I would return to repeatedly as I continued taking leaps of faith and creating a life that felt right for me. I had to practice surrender when I made a significant investment in a financial program to help me build my independence and grow my financial literacy, when I hired a coach to help me take steps toward building my own business, and when I left a secure 9-to-5 career to write my first book and pursue a full-time living in writing and speaking. Time and time again, I took heart-led, calculated risks to create the authentic life that was calling me. And with each step came its own version of the free fall or freak-out moment when I questioned what I was doing. Each leap also grew my trust and taught me how to live in a state of surrender. I would remind myself, *This isn't falling. You're safe. It's just the feeling of flying before the chute opens.* Some days, I would have to remind myself of this over and over again, but eventually, I found a rhythm. I would breathe, loosen my grip, and lean back into the trust and faith that had carried me this far. Here, I'd find my peace again.

Surrender has taught me that I can trust myself and my decisions. I can trust in a higher power supporting me, and I can trust that good things are always coming, no matter what I face along the way. My trust has grown as I've seen dreams and visions come to fruition on the other side of my leaps. Much like I discovered in college, the Universe has a way of surprising us with blessings far greater than we could have imagined if we're willing to let go of control and make room for them.

If you find yourself standing on the edge of a leap, I invite you to surrender. Let go of the need to control or know exactly how it's going to unfold, and trust the nudge that's been tugging at your heart. Know that when you leap, you're not falling; you're soaring into the life that's been waiting for you all along. And if you've already leaped, remember to breathe, loosen your grip, and allow the wind to take you. When fear and doubt rush in, remind yourself that the free fall is temporary. Trust the process; trust yourself. Open your arms and fly.

PRACTICAL APPLICATION

A Moment of Surrender

Heart/God/Universe (whatever feels right for you),

Thank you for your help and guidance throughout my journey. I trust that I am not alone. I let go of my worries and my doubts. I release the urge to control it all. I surrender my plan and open myself up to something far greater. Thank you for all the good things in my life today and for all the blessings on the way.

CHAPTER 15

BLISS

Follow your bliss and the universe will open doors where there were only walls.
−*Joseph Campbell*

I didn't know I could experience the level of joy and freedom that I feel in my life today. There are so many moments where I pause and ask myself, *Is this really the life I'm living?* On the other side of my leap has been everything I've wanted and more. I've found love with another person that brings my heart and my life so much joy. I've found contentment and acceptance within myself that has brought incredible peace. And I've discovered the freedom that comes when you face your fears and allow yourself to pursue the life you're meant for.

This past year, my partner and I had the opportunity to take our first trip to Hawaii together. We spent a day on the beautiful beaches of the North Shore, then found our way to Waimea Falls. We took a short hike through what felt like a Hawaiian jungle to reach the waterfall. There was beauty surrounding us on every side: huge, towering trees, flowers we'd never seen before, and Monstera leaves half our size, climbing to the sky.

We had planned to just look at the waterfall because we were short on time and had to head back for dinner, but everyone knows you can't go to a waterfall and just look—you have to get in. Instead of waiting in a long line for life jackets, my partner was resourceful and grabbed two from a couple as they were getting out of the falls. We quickly slipped them on and made our way to the water. My body shivered as soon as my toes touched the water. It was cold but refreshing at the same time. I let myself sink in and felt the cool water embrace me. I looked up at my partner, who was ahead of me, with a huge smile on her face. She said, "We have to put our heads under the waterfall."

We made our way over, and as we got closer, the mist began to kiss our faces and arms. We put our heads under the water as the fall drenched our faces, reminding us of what it feels like to be alive. I began letting go and became fully present in the moment. I raised my head slightly out of the water and looked up. The sun was glistening through the fall, creating a moment that couldn't be duplicated or captured in words. It was all breathtaking. We started to make our way back, and I paused. I looked my partner in the eyes and felt a rush of gratitude overwhelm me. I couldn't believe we were here. Not just in a waterfall in Hawaii but in this place in our life together. This moment of pure presence, bliss, and joy encapsulated what this journey has been like for us. While it hasn't been perfect or always easy, the joy we've found and the life we're building are worth every second of it. This moment in Hawaii was even better than I had imagined, and this leap has led me to a life that's even better than I could have envisioned.

On the other side of my leap, I've found bliss, joy, and freedom. It's a life more beautiful than I ever thought it could be. I'm still building this life every day and navigating the ups and downs we all face, but the joy I've experienced has made it all so worth it.

My leap has taught me that when you follow your heart, trust your intuition, lean into faith, push past discomfort, and courageously go after what you desire, good things will be on the other side. Remember, life bends for the courageous. Everything you're longing for is available to you; you just have to let go and be willing to take a bold leap of faith.

CHAPTER 16

YOUR TIME TO FLY

What if I fall? Oh, but my darling, what if you fly?
-Erin Hanson

What if, one year from now, your life looks completely different? What if you are living your dreams, experiencing more joy than ever, and fully at peace in your own skin? Imagine feeling confident, fearless, and surrounded by deep, meaningful relationships. What if you are thriving in your dream career and doing work that fulfills you? What if the desires you've been too afraid to voice finally come to life? What if you step fully into the authentic life that's been calling you all along?

Anything is possible when you embrace your courage and take the leap.

My journey was about more than just creating new circumstances in my life. It was about stepping into a new version of myself. The "me" that's been there all along, just waiting to be fully embraced and brought into the world. These were the words I wrote when I started this process:

> I no longer settle in any area of my life. I go after my dreams with my whole heart. I finally let go of the fear of disappointing others and the weight of not being enough. I've stepped into the real me. I feel confident in my own skin. I embrace her, the real Danielle. I love her fully. I am ready to take bold steps of faith toward my purpose and live the life of my dreams.

Reflecting back on this now, I realize…

This is who I've become.

The life I'm creating is beautiful, but what may be even more attractive is the person I've become along the way. Embracing your authenticity and taking leaps toward a life that aligns with your truth is a journey of acceptance, surrender, and profound transformation. Don't be surprised if you find yourself changed on the other side of this process. I would go so far as to say that's the whole point: to embrace the truest version of who you are, so you can live the fullest life available to you.

You now have everything you need to LEAP.

Listen to your heart.

Embrace your faith

Accept your truth.

Pursue your path.

Before you put this book down, I encourage you to ask yourself one more time:

What do I want?

Close your eyes.

See it.

Feel it.

Believe it's already yours.

I will leave you with this:

Don't settle for a life that doesn't light your soul on fire. Don't settle for a life that you will look back on and regret one day. Don't settle for anything less than what your heart desires.

You are worthy of a beautiful, abundant life—a life filled with love, peace, and endless joy.

There is so much waiting for you on the other side. Be Brave. Be bold.

Take the leap.

TAKE IT A STEP FURTHER

The LEAP Course

A Guided Journey to Your Authentic Life

Whether you're just beginning *Take the Leap* or ready to go even deeper, this online course is here to support your transformation every step of the way.

In this self-paced experience, author Danielle Bongiorno expands on the powerful LEAP Method—guiding you through the same four-step process to go from feeling stuck or uncertain to living with clarity, courage, and alignment.

Inside the course, you'll find:

Coaching videos to deepen your insight

Guided meditations to help you connect inward

Reflective exercises and tools to support your journey

If you're ready to trust yourself, take bold steps, and create a life that feels true to you—this is your next move.

Visit the link or scan the QR code below to begin:

leapcourse.daniellebongiorno.com

SHARE YOUR THOUGHTS

Leave a Review

Was this book meaningful to you?

If *Take the Leap* spoke to your heart, would you take a moment to share your experience?

Leaving a review on Amazon helps this message reach more people who are searching for the same kind of clarity, courage, and freedom.

Even a few words can make a big difference.

Visit the link or scan the QR code below to leave your review:

bookreview.daniellebongiorno.com

REFERENCES

1   Ware, Bronnie. 2019. *The Top Five Regrets of Dying.* Hay House.

2   Nguyen, Joseph. 2022. *Don't Believe Everything You Think.* One Satori.

3   LePera, Dr. Nicole n.d. *The Holistic Psychologist.* https://theholisticpsychologist.com/how-to-do-ego-work/.

4   LePera, Dr. Nicole. December 17, 2023. *The Holistic Psychologist.* https://www.youtube.com/watch?v=3tUQnhRi0J8.

5   Hanh, Thich Nhat. 2001. *You are Here.* Shamnhala Publications.

6   Nguyen, Joseph. 2022. *Don't Believe Everything You Think.* One Satori.

7   LePera, Dr. Nicole. March 7, 2025. *The Holistic Psychologist.* https://www.youtube.com/shorts/BJdjz52plNs.

8   LePera, Dr. Nicole. July 6, 2024. *The Holistic Psychologist.* https://www.youtube.com/watch?v=WExXuO0xxYM.

9   Menigoz, Wendy, Tracy T. Latz, Robin A. Ely, Cimone Kamei, Gregory Melvin, and Drew Sinatra. 2020. *Integrative and lifestyle medicine strategies should include Earthing (grounding): Review of research evidence and clinical observations.* https://www.sciencedirect.com/science/article/pii/S1550830719305476.

10 Ortner, Nick. n.d. *The Ultimate Guide to the Gamut Point in EFT Tapping: Everything You Need to Know.* https://www.thetappingsolution.com/blog/gamut-point/.

11 van der Kolk, Bessel A. 2014. *The Body Keeps the Score.* Viking.

12 All Points North. November 15, 2021. *Fight, Flight, Freeze, Fawn, and Flop: Responses to Trauma.* https://apn.com/resources/fight-flight-freeze-fawn-and-flop-responses-to-trauma/.

13 LePera, Dr. Nicole. December 3, 2024. *The Holistic Psychologist.* https://youtube.com/shorts/uHYo79cV5Ok?si=C0LJs3nQedVuhVQt.

14 Virtue Ph.D., Doreen. 2005. *Angel Numbers.* Hay House.

15   Innes, LJ. December 20, 2017. *The Meaning of a Deer Sighting.* https://www.californiapsychics.com/blog/animal-sightings-symbolism/meaning-deer-sighting.html.

16   Fauna. October 12, 2022. *Deer spirit animal: Symbolism and meaning.* https://fauna-protect.com/en-us/blogs/spirit-animals/spirit-animal-deer.

17   Love to Know. March 4, 2025. *Love to Know.* https://www.lovetoknow.com/life/lifestyle/spiritual-meaning-rainbow.

18   Pierson, Judith. 2022. "The Power of the Subconscious Mind." *Research Gate.* November. https://www.researchgate.net/publication/365211107_The_Power_of_the_Subconscious_Mind.

19   LePera, Dr. Nicole. 2021. *How to Do the Work.* Harper Collins.

20   Brown, Brené 2007. *I Thought It Was Just Me (but it isn't).* Avery.

21   Brown, Brené. 2010. *The Gifts of Imperfection.* Hazeldon Publishing.

22   Brown, Brené. 2015. *Daring Greatly.* Avery.

23   Fairchild, Alana. 2015. *Sacred Rebels Oracle: Guidance for Living a Unique & Authentic Life.* Llewellyn Publications.

GRATITUDE

To my parents, Frank and Rushell, thank you for your unconditional love and unwavering support through every leap and chapter of my journey. From my days on the basketball court to now, you've always been in my corner, cheering me on and believing in me. I love you so much.

To my sisters, Jess and Kenz, for always being there and standing by me through every season of life. Whether I need someone to talk to, a good laugh, or help picking out an outfit, I know I can always count on you both. Thank you for loving every version of me. I truly don't know what I'd do without you.

To my niece, Elly, for encouraging me to be my true self and follow my heart, and to my nephews, Memphis and Grey, and brother-in-law, Christian, for loving me just as I am.

To my partner, Camille, for the countless hours you spent helping me behind the scenes, reading drafts, answering questions, and patiently listening. Thank you for believing in me since day one and encouraging me to keep going, even on my hardest days. I love you so much, and I'm so grateful to be on this journey with you.

To Taryn, for being a consistent and loyal friend, a sounding board, and the safe space I needed when this journey began. Thank you for seeing me.

To Casey, our conversation on the porch that day in Lake Tahoe is a moment I won't forget and became a launching pad for this book-writing journey. Thank you for lovingly calling me forward and helping me find the courage to take the step my heart was calling me toward.

To my dear friends Kevin, Aaron, Becky, and Gina, thank you for reading early drafts, offering thoughtful feedback, and above all, believing in my vision and encouraging me to keep going.

To my coaches, mentors, and healers who have walked with me through so many stages of my journey. Justin, Scott, Sara, Elizabeth, and Ana, thank you for holding space, offering guidance, and helping me become the woman I am today.

To Darnah Mercieca, my publishing strategist, for your guidance, belief, and steady presence that helped bring this book to life.

To my editors, Cailin Porter and Alice Visinand, for your care, insight, and feedback that helped shape the book into what it is today.

To my sister, Kenz Bongiorno, for bringing my cover vision to life with her original illustration, and to my cover designer, Alannah Graham, for thoughtfully creating the finished piece.

To all of the family and friends who have cheered me on through your encouragement, belief, or financial support. I'm so grateful.

And to my Mema, who I know is looking down on me and so proud of me for living a life that makes me truly happy.

I couldn't have done this without all of you.

ABOUT THE AUTHOR

Danielle Bongiorno is an author, speaker, and coach who has taken bold steps to face her fears, reshape her path, and live with greater freedom and purpose. Through her writing and speaking, she inspires others to trust their hearts, embrace courage, and create lives they truly love.

Danielle's story is one of resilience, vulnerability, and reinvention. She began her career coaching and mentoring female athletes before transitioning into the corporate world, where she quickly rose to senior director. Despite checking all the boxes of success, she couldn't shake the feeling that she wasn't living true to herself. In her 30s, she took a bold leap toward authenticity by coming out and fully embracing her sexuality. That courageous choice sparked a profound transformation, inspiring her to follow her heart in every area of her life. She eventually walked away from her 9-to-5 to pursue her dream of becoming an author and speaker—on a mission to inspire others to live fearlessly and own their truth.

Danielle's message is simple: don't settle, trust your heart, and when life nudges you… *take the leap*.

When she's not writing or speaking, you'll find her exploring new cities with her partner, walking at the beach with their Golden Retriever, or soaking in live music.

Learn more at www.daniellebongiorno.com

www.ingramcontent.com/pod-product-compliance
Lightning Source LLC
Chambersburg PA
CBHW031436120626
46545CB00006B/2427